To Mary and [...]
Another [...]
collector! But it is
very [...] to have
authors send [...]
inscribed copies —

To two old friends —
with whom many joyous
and not so wonderful —
events were shared —
and who will Therefore
find it both miraculous
and funny, as I do to
be an author of a book!
love —
Ruth

# SOCIAL AGENCY STRUCTURE AND ACCOUNTABILITY:

A Case Study of the
Arthur Lehman Counseling Service

# SOCIAL AGENCY STRUCTURE AND ACCOUNTABILITY

A Case Study of
the Arthur Lehman
Counseling Service

by
RUTH FIZDALE

Introduction by
KATHARINE D. HARVEY

R. E. BURDICK, Inc. *publishers*
Fair Lawn, New Jersey 07410, U.S.A.

International Standard Book Number: 0-913638-06-4
Library of Congress Catalogue Card Number: 74-79259

Published by R. E. Burdick, Inc.,
12-01 12th Street, Fair Lawn, New Jersey 07410

Published simultaneously in Canada
by the Book Center, Inc.,
1140 Beaulac Street, Montreal, Quebec H4R 1R8

Printed in the United States of America

# CONTENTS

# PREFACE

THE GREATEST difficulty in constructing this report came in the selection of significant content. Having undertaken to conduct a pilot venture on behalf of social work, it was logical that we report on its outcome. But the venture had hardly begun when social work colleagues began to raise pertinent questions: Why should a social agency serve the rich? How was a service of high quality assured clients if practitioners carried sole accountability for service given? These and other questions, obviously of importance to others, required answers. At the same time we needed to share what seemed like a revelation to us in being confronted in a nonphilanthropic setting with the degree to which the philanthropic origins of social work have influenced the development of our profession: our values, the services we offer, the very way in which they are offered, and the conflictual nature of some of these influences with professional roles and responsibilities. Social work is philanthropy's child at precisely that point in its life where it must establish its own identity as a profession—not as philanthropy. Like any child at this stage, it is struggling with the dilemma of choosing which of the parental characteristics to retain, where to assert its differences, and how

to deal with the problems of separation without repu-
diation. Our own experiences with these conflicts seemed
important to report.

I hope that the foci selected will be responsive to the
anticipated interests of others in social work and to the
questions they subsequently raised, and that they will be
provocative of further dialogue concerning the nature of
social work's professional role in society and the education
required for this role.

The Arthur Lehman Counseling Service was truly the
product of collaborative effort. Professional staff (social
workers and consultants), clerical staff and the Technical
Advisory Committee were equally committed to a common
goal. What evolved could not have been accomplished without the vision of our founding group regarding the significance of social work's recognition as a profession and without their confidence in it. Nor could we have achieved what
we did without the founding group's profound understanding of the nature of experimentation; without the Board of
Directors' recognition of a professional person's need for
autonomy if he is to fulfill his professional role soundly
and with a sense of integrity. Achievement would also have
been impossible without the practitioner staff's commitment to a high level of professional service as primary in
seeking recognition as a profession, and impossible without
an intelligent and involved clerical staff, who came to share
our common mission. Neither could anything have been
accomplished without the commitment of our Technical
Advisory Committee, apparent in the help they gave initially; in their willingness to face some of the meaning of
our experience as it developed, to encourage testing out of
ideas; and in their maintaining the role of catalysts, asking
the not always popular question, making the necessary comments essential for accountability to our profession. To say

thank you to any one of these groups or to persons within them would be to deny the very essence of the project—a collaborative relationship to which each person brought his special experience and knowledge and used them toward the achievement of a common objective.

However, I do believe that thanks are due from the profession of social work to the founders of ALCS—Mrs. Richard J. Bernhard, Mrs. Benjamin J. Buttenwieser, Mrs. Arthur Lehman, Mrs. John L. Loeb, Dr. Maurice B. Hexter, and Mr. Ira M. Younker; to the Adele and Arthur Lehman Foundation; and to all the members of the Board of Directors of ALCS. All of them were well ahead of most social workers in understanding the potential significance of our public recognition as a profession. However, what was of even greater importance was their courage and willingness to take a then not widely accepted step while we in the profession were hesitant and uncertain and reluctant to take on the risks involved. To these persons I believe social work is deeply indebted for their courage to put their convictions to public test and thus help us move to a greater self- and public identification as a profession and through this to a more responsible role in the provision of services needed by all clients and communities.

In producing the report itself, I am grateful to several individuals and wish to acknowledge my indebtedness to them. My primary thanks go to Mrs. Barbara B. Frank, who carried over to me from her job as office manager and secretary the same unusual capacity to be a partner in the truest sense of the word. I am particularly grateful to her for her ability to be responsive to and identify with my frustrations as an author, yet stay related to the objective, maintaining a separateness while sustaining me in my commitment to completing this report. I also wish to thank Mrs. Elinor P. Zaki, whose intimate knowledge of ALCS since its inception and whose considerable skill as an editor have made this report clear and readable. I also wish to thank Mrs. Harold D. Harvey and Mr. Lawrence B. Buttenwieser, who in their separate and characteristic fashions gave me the support needed to complete this task.

RUTH FIZDALE

# INTRODUCTION

THE PASSAGE of more than twenty years does not seem to have dimmed for me the memory of the establishment and early years of the Arthur Lehman Counseling Service. It was an exciting experience for me, and though I do not speak officially for my fellow board members, I believe it to have been true for them also. We were together in a venture that dealt with ideas important to us all. My acceptance of Dorothy Lehman Bernhard's invitation to help launch the pilot project was based to some extent on my admiration for and faith in that wise and energetic leader in the field of social welfare. In addition, my faith in the profession of social work made me respond enthusiastically to the idea behind the venture proposed.

The feeling of excitement never wholly left me, but all of us involved shared other emotions—bewilderment, doubt, frustration, as well as the satisfaction that comes with achievement. The important thing was that we were involved. It was almost impossible to be unconcerned about the innovations, the difficulties and the progress. Board members knew from the start that they would not be responsible for raising funds for the program, and it was assumed that they would use their considerable experience in social welfare to be responsive to the voice and needs of the community they hoped to serve, making decisions for the agency based on those responses and assuming other and quite usual duties of advisory committees that work with a director chosen by the board. Eventually we came to realize that the nature of ALCS demanded reexamination of the place of the board in the agency that was emerging. It is my belief that the board's most significant contributions to ALCS came when it saw itself collaborating with, rather than advising, the staff. I would not claim that the board's adjustment to this role was complete, but the effort was always challenging.

That the agency lived and prospered through its pilot period and beyond is due in great measure to its director. She helped the board to recognize the ways in which the agency could achieve its ends and to facilitate the necessary changes without disruption. The members of the Technical Advisory Committee were glad to have an opportunity to be close to a new agency with goals in which they believed but which were different from those of their own agencies. The director kept them in touch with the project and with tact and skill helped them to see where their constructive advice and criticism would be most useful. The ingenuity with which she used her relationship with the staff will be appreciated by those who read between the lines in the report that follows. Ruth Fizdale, firm in her convictions about the philosophy and practice of social work, joined staff, board and advisors in searching for the methods that would best steer ALCS toward its goals.

I succumb to the temptation to make some personal observations because they may help the reader to sense some of the underlying dynamics of the ALCS program. The experience of working collaboratively with a group consisting exclusively of highly trained and experienced casework practitioners, top level executives and lay persons with long and varied experience in social welfare for me was challenging, educational and productive. Responsibilities and relationships were viewed in a new light which forced me to see that long-accepted policies and procedures were not immutable but could be made more appropriate to the social agency of today. It was salutory to have to relearn some fundamental truths about the democratic process. Probably all of us in ALCS experienced at one time or another some difficulty in adjusting to new roles. It was not always easy for the board to accept the fact that its authority in this agency did not derive from representation of funding sources. On the other hand, staff learned that *they* were responsible for the solvency of the agency and had to assume duties which, as employees in other agencies, had been decided and carried out for them. Always, however, it was stimulating to be part of a project that became increasingly an object of interest--whether skeptical or approving—to the field of social work; a project that was opening new vistas for people in need of counseling, for agencies, schools of social work, and other professions.

In an even more personal vein I want to express the gratitude I owe to two persons with whom I worked closely in ALCS. Dorothy Bernhard demonstrated that the need we all have to help others must be satisfied through thoughtful, practical and imaginative use of resources and by blending one's own personality and convictions with those of others. Through the years of her presidency and after, these qualities illuminated the agency and helped us all to use effectively the grant so wisely provided by her family.

After becoming president of ALCS, I worked far more closely with Ruth Fizdale. She was painstaking and patient in helping me to see the agency as a whole and to see what the president's contribution could be and to see that the "how" is often more important than the "what." She helped me to clarify my thoughts and premises, to modify them and to use them constructively, and I gained immeasurably from our frequent discussions. My gratitude to Dorothy Bernhard and Ruth Fizdale reflects, I am sure, that of all who had the privilege of working with them.

A report or "case history" on ALCS was contemplated early. Like much else in the history of the agency, the form it was to take was not planned in advance. In a sense it planned itself as it became clear that what was most important in the ALCS experience was not so much the results as the steps that led to them. A strict evaluation could best have been made by a person not involved in the agency. A critical examination of methods, procedure and sequences could only be made by painstaking search through written material and intimacy with personalities and events. ALCS was very fortunate in selecting its director and equally fortunate in keeping her services to the end. That she had the objectivity and skill to bring together in a report pertinent facts and figures, as well as to select significant points of movement, made it clear to the board that Ruth Fizdale was the logical person to write its history.

The document that follows was prepared for lay and professional persons responsible for continuing evaluation of what and how services are provided for their clients and for those with a continuing responsibility for educating lay and professional persons for their roles. This report is being presented in fulfillment of the self-imposed responsibility of the ALCS board and staff, implicit in their having undertaken a pilot venture on behalf of the profession of social work.

KATHARINE D. HARVEY

# 1. The Aims of ALCS and Its Administrative Structure

IN 1954 the Arthur Lehman Counseling Service opened its doors for the purpose of reaching and serving persons who previously had not availed themselves materially of casework services. The target population can roughly be described as those in the middle-income and upper-income socioeconomic groups. ALCS set itself the task of testing, on behalf of the profession of social work, whether this target group would use the counseling services of caseworkers under any conditions or would turn only to other professions, such as psychiatry and psychology, for counseling services. If this group were successfully reached, ALCS would provide the profession with information about the conditions under which casework services should be offered, what services beyond counseling would be required and, finally, what additional costs communities would need to meet if they wanted to serve this group and whether the fees charged could not cover the cost of service of high caliber.

Behind this pilot [1] experiment venture lay the desire of the founding group to remove a serious obstacle to the social work profession in its struggle to be heard and to have its competence and knowledge recognized and used effectively by legislators, social planners, and communities. Social work's historical commitment to serve the economically deprived had led a substantial portion of the general public to view social workers as champions of the disadvantaged, rather than as knowledgeable and skilled members of an emerging profession. Their recommendations on social planning consequently were often by-passed as merely the biased views of "do-gooders." This distorted impression of social work discouraged the public from giving financial support to what the social work profession advocated as essential social welfare programs. Similarly ignored were social work's recommendations concerning research and the training essential for the improvement of social services. Moreover, the public's view of social work did not foster the full use of casework services by those persons who, though economically advantaged, also needed help with family and personal problems. Too few people believed that

> The...skilled assistance of the caseworker is of value not only to the lower income groups, but equally to those who find that a substantial income does not assure a happy marriage, a confident child, or a carefree old age. [2]

The founders of ALCS [3] believed that if social caseworkers were able to reach and serve the middle- and upper-income groups, the public's understanding and concept of the social work profession would change for the better. They believed that if these persons—whose relationships to social agencies had been chiefly as contributors to and providers of service—could themselves receive the benefits of this professional service, they would not only understand it better but also would be more likely to support high standards of service, training and research. As a consequence, the professional service to *all* clients would improve. [4]  The founders of ALCS pointed to the history of hospital care as evidence of the validity of this hypothesis. Subsequent to the opening of private and semiprivate pavilions, donations were received from the general public for better equipment, for research and for higher standards of medical care in general. As a result, all hospital patients, clinic and ward patients, as well as those under private care, benefited.

The idea behind the establishment of ALCS was not entirely new. In 1942, the Jewish Family Service of New York opened its Consultation Center, based on the belief that the social work profession possessed skills and knowledge that could be used by people in all walks of life. [5] JFS believed that proving the validity of this idea meant that social work would have to meet the test of the "marketplace" by charging a fee for social casework service. JFS thus took the first step away from the profession's *total* identification with the economically disadvantaged and with philanthropic purposes. Its fees, however, were based on a sliding scale, according to the client's ability to pay. Therefore, the misconception that social work could be useful solely to persons with economic problems was only partially dispelled.

But the JFS undertaking did leave an indelible impression on the profession of social work. Its fee-charging program was copied by agencies across the United States. One has but to read the social work literature of the 1940s and 1950s to see the effect these programs had on the profession's knowledge and skills. [6] Unfortunately, they had little impact on the *public's* general concept of social work as a profession. One may wonder, for example, to what extent the policy of determining the fee on the basis of a client's ability to pay helped obscure the message that social work is a profession and that its services are of value to persons in all economic and social strata.

The private practice of social work had predated even

the JFS program. [7]   Private practitioners did serve the economically advantaged. The fees they charged were based on their estimate of reasonable compensation for their training and experience. However, they also had little effect on the public's understanding of professional social work, perhaps because they were few in number and some of them did not identify themselves as social workers. Moreover, the professional organization did not recognize them as social work practitioners. Through its formal structure, the social work profession expressed the belief that social work could not be practiced outside an institutional setting.

Thus it was that the question concerning the general public's potential acceptance of social work as a profession was still unanswered in 1954, when ALCS was established. Finding the answer seemed to lie, in part at least, in offering a social work service on the same terms as those set by other professions. One of the usual terms set by other professions is that a fee should be charged, and that the fee set by the professional person should represent adequate compensation for the time required to prepare himself for practice and for his subsequent experience leading to the acquisition of skill and competence. Offering service for a fee determined in this way would provide a basis for testing social work in the "marketplace." The service selected by ALCS for such testing was social casework counseling. Would the target clientele seek and pay for social casework counseling if the fee were substantial and nonphilanthropic? What would be the result if the fee were competitive with the fees charged by other professions offering counseling and psychotherapeutic services? Was social work, indeed, as many thought, only the poor man's psychiatry or therapy?

These were among the questions the founders of ALCS undertook to explore on behalf of social work, through the pilot program undertaken in New York City. Beginning in 1952, they discussed the idea with leading social workers in the field. In 1953, they requested the Adele and Arthur Lehman Foundation to grant funds sufficient to set up an agency with a dual purpose: *1) to offer family and individual casework counseling under conditions that would attract a middle- and upper-income clientele; 2) to undertake the responsibility of reporting the agency's experience to social agencies and interested lay and professional leaders in communities throughout the United States.* The hope was that, if warranted, similar programs would be initiated elsewhere. Such expansion would be essential if the goal of establishing social casework counseling as a professional discipline in the eyes of the general public were to be achieved.

The founders asked for a grant large enough to support the pilot program for a period of five to ten years. It was their belief that this would provide enough time to determine whether the target clientele would use social casework services and to find the answers to other questions concerning services to this group which lay and professional social work leaders would need in determining the future relationship of social agencies and social workers to economically advantaged clients. It was their further hope that, if the pilot program did reach a new clientele, the family agencies in New York City would assume responsibility for expanding their own programs to serve them. The major aims of ALCS would then have been achieved and the organization could go out of existence, after making a final report to the profession.

The Adele and Arthur Lehman Foundation made the grant requested, and the founders became the core group on the Board of Directors, which also included other lay and professional leaders. The service to be offered by ALCS was defined by the founding core of the board as *family and individual counseling.* No other services usual to family agencies were to be given. Ruth Fizdale was hired as Executive Director to begin work on January 15, 1954.

Offices were acquired in a brownstone building in a semi-residential area in April, 1954. They were attractively furnished, conveying a sense of a comfortable and friendly professional office. Each room was air-conditioned, in itself an unusual comfort for social agency clients and staff in 1954. The waiting room gave clients a sense of privacy. A modest campaign of advance information to the public was begun, consisting primarily of an effort to inform leaders in the fields of medicine, law, psychology, social work, religion, and education of the aims of the new agency. News releases were issued at the time the office was opened, making clear that the counseling services, now offered on a nonphilanthropic basis, were identical with such services offered by social agencies to persons who could not afford full-cost fees.

*The Three Phases in the Life of ALCS*

There were (as it later became evident) three phases through which ALCS passed during its existence. The first was the pilot phase which ended around the end of 1957 and the beginning of 1958. The second phase, best defined as the interim period, extended roughly from 1958 to 1960. The final phase lasted from 1960 through December, 1969, when the client service was taken over by the Park East Counseling Group.

It is always difficult to know when a pilot program is over. New questions emerge that are of equal interest to board and staff and can become confused with initial goals. Additional data are being acquired. Findings that could have been summarized earlier are strengthened. Thus it was only in reviewing the minutes in preparing to write this report that it became apparent that the original pilot questions were answered by and large by the end of 1957. It is now obvious that 1958 was the beginning of a new phase, in which some conclusion to the pilot program was sought.

During this interim phase there was deep concern about ALCS responsibility for encouraging others (social agencies and leaders in the field of social welfare) to open similar services. The family agencies represented on our Technical Advisory Committee joined in discussing the possibility of their taking over responsibility for the client group we had reached. We asked the staff to consider the values of a group practice and whether they were interested in forming one. Board members questioned the need for their continued participation and whether a board had any role in an agency wholly supported by client fees. And the Administrative Committee undertook to review what had been accomplished to date.

In 1960, it was decided that if ALCS could be fully self-supporting, it would be set up as a permanent agency in New York City. This decision marked the beginning of the final phase. Concern was then focused on the structure required for an agency (not a pilot demonstration) that would be self-supporting and would have a highly experienced staff. What changes in structure would the new type of agency require if it were to achieve its purpose? It is not surprising that at the time ALCS was passing through each of these phases, they were viewed as next steps in their pilot program. Each phase had characteristics of innovation, which will become clearer later in this report.

In the description of the structure that follows, the hypotheses and the characteristics of each of these three phases will be set forth. The reader may find this method of presentation somewhat difficult to follow, but it was purposely chosen because it illuminates *the process of change*. It highlights the recognition of strain and of problems, the seeking of resolution, the inherent difficulties of overcoming the pull of tradition in the process of readjustment to a new situation, and the difficulty of maintaining consistency, particularly at points of crisis. It is hoped that presenting the material in this sequential and detailed manner will help other social agencies to move more quickly and with less trial and error in opening similar services. The more one is aware of the *course* of change, the easier it is to achieve the desired readjustment.

## The Administrative Structure [8]

The administrative structure of an agency reflects its aims—immediate and long-range—and its conception of its accountability. It reflects not only to whom the agency is accountable, but for what it is accountable and which unit of the agency will carry which elements of accountability. The roles and responsibilities assigned to the component units and the channels of communication established within and among them are predicated on the achievement of agency aims and fulfillment of agency accountability. What were some of the hypotheses underlying the structure evolved in ALCS?

It must be remembered that ALCS began as a somewhat innovative agency and as a pilot demonstration. In its initial phase, therefore, its structure could not be the same as that of an established social agency. The structure evolved was based on certain hypotheses about the client group to be reached, the accountability of a pilot demonstration, and the relationship between the administrator and the practitioner staff.

Concerning the client group to be reached, three hypotheses were advanced about the conditions under which they might avail themselves of social casework services: 1) it would be necessary to establish a fee that was non-philanthropic in character, since the target clientele, in seeking other professional services, had been accustomed to having the fee set by the professional practitioner; 2) it would be necessary that the person offering service to this group be a professional practitioner with full training and substantial experience; 3) these clients would expect that service would be given in pleasant, professional surroundings.

It was further hypothesized that, as a pilot project, ALCS would be primarily accountable to the profession of social work. In accountability, a pilot program is more akin to a research project than to a social service agency. Social agencies offering direct services are actually accountable to three "communities": 1) the donor community, or the source of income, voluntary or governmental; 2) the client community, the persons on whose behalf the service has been developed; and 3) the professional community, whose values, knowledge and skills shape the service offered and are shaped by social agency experience. In its accountability to the donor community, a social agency must account, on a continuing basis, for the use of funds granted or being requested. The board, viewed as representing the donor community, is trusted to protect donor interests and to use funds economically in providing services for clients. In this respect, a social agency is different from a pilot project which, like a research project, in a sense will have completed its accountability to the donor group when the grant has been approved. Grants for pilot projects and research are given because, in the opinion of the grantor, the idea is worth exploring regardless of its outcome, and the persons to whom the grant has been given are considered competent to carry out the project. A pilot program, therefore, is primarily accountable to the profession on whose behalf the testing of an idea is undertaken. It must answer to the profession for its "findings." In this process, the profession holds the professional staff accountable as it examines methodology and design (which includes staff qualifications, costs involved, as well as roles and responsibilities assigned), as well as for the recommendations and conclusions drawn from the experience. Inherent in any professional undertaking, of course, is accountability to the clients served.

Lastly, it was assumed that a sound pilot venture would require a "team relationship" between the executive and the practitioner staff. One of our aims was, understandably, to hear and evaluate the expectations of the new client group. The practitioner's firsthand contact with the client, his understanding of the intricacies of treatment and their relation to client expectations were seen as enriching the conduct of the pilot program. The practitioner's direct contact with clients would add depth to the executive's broad perspective of the pilot experience. It was hypothesized that the achievement of a team relationship depended upon the practitioners' carrying full responsibility for their direct service to clients. To be accountable to the *executive* for their practice would hinder their ability to function as peers in the conduct of the pilot program. Moreover, it was hypothesized that the quality of client service is likely to be higher if the practitioner feels he is directly responsible to his clients and does not share this responsibility with a supervisor or an administrator.

In the discussion that follows, each component unit of the administrative structure, with its particular roles, responsibilities and relationships, will be dealt with separately.

## 1.  The Board of Directors

ALCS began its pilot demonstration with the traditional concept of the need for a Board of Directors. The board members were selected somewhat in accordance with tradition in New York City for a non-sectarian agency, with representatives of the three major sectarian groups—Protestant, Catholic, and Jewish. The criteria for selection were not wholly traditional, however, and were based in part on what was thought to be necessary for the sound conduct of the pilot program. The primary criteria for selection were long experience in social agencies and the social welfare field, either as members of boards of directors or as consultants and practitioners; conviction that social casework is a professional discipline in its own right, and that there is value in establishing social work as a profession in the eyes of the public; and willingness to make a commitment of from five to ten years, or until some disposition had been made for the provision of parallel services to the target client group. These criteria were set by the founding core of the Board of Directors, but were accepted by later members as the board expanded.

Prospective board members were asked about their interest in the aims of the pilot program and the invitation placed emphasis on the advisory role for this board. This was implied in their being informed that they would have *no* fund-raising responsibilities, since the Lehman Foundation grant was sufficient to cover all operating costs of a client service and of whatever experimentation was essential to achieve the pilot aims. They were assured that there would be little if any committee work. Instead, their advice would be sought on an individual basis as issues arose in which their special experience and knowledge would be relevant. Nothing was said to indicate that the board would not carry final responsibility for policy decisions. It was assumed that they would, but that the process of arriving at decisions would be different than in other social agencies having a continuous problem of funding and boards comprised of persons with varying degrees of experience. It was assumed that highly experienced and knowledgeable board members would have few differences of opinion on policy matters, either among themselves or with experienced professionals. Freed from the problems of funding, their mutuality in goals and in ideas would come to the fore, making for free exchange and easy arrival at policy decisions.

Provision was made for a minimum of four full board meetings a year. An Administrative Committee to meet on a monthly basis or as frequently as necessary was also established. This committee consisted of the Chairman of the board, the President, the Vice President, the Secretary, the Treasurer, and two to three members-at-large. It was initially elected by the board in 1954 and reelected each year for a period of ten years. Although some changes did occur in this committee, they were few and occasioned by the personal situations of the committee members. Similarly, once appointed to the board, each member's term of office was the period required to achieve the goals of the pilot project. The underlying principle was that board stability and continuity were essential for a pilot program. No nominating committee was established. The few additional members appointed between 1954 and 1962 were informally proposed by one or another board member at a board meeting, were approached by a member of the Administrative Committee, and the results were presented to the board for information or approval.

The Administrative Committee served as a clearinghouse for all staff [9] recommendations concerning the design of the pilot program and its counseling services: staffing patterns; qualifications for professional and clerical staff and consultants; personnel practices, including salaries, and so forth. This committee reviewed proposals and, if approved, presented them to the board for consideration and final approval. Votes were rarely necessary since consensus usually was apparent. The Administrative Committee decided when the board needed to be informed of a decision and when its review was required.

Between 1954 and 1961 individual members of the board were consulted between meetings. One was the regular consultant on relationships with private schools, another on relationships with clergy and others were consulted in relation to financial questions.

Throughout the pilot and interim phases of the agency, the Executive Director served as the link and the avenue of exchange between the board and staff. Other staff members did not attend board or Administrative Committee meetings, but the Executive Director conveyed to the committee and the board their recommendations, advice and interests. Similarly, she informed the staff of board requests and decisions.

This definition of board role and responsibilities and method of exchange continued throughout the pilot program and began to create some difficulties during the interim phase, but only in regard to fiscal matters. In the final phase (1962 on), however, several changes were instituted. A Nominating Committee was appointed as a standing committee. For an ongoing agency such as ALCS had become, some system of handling additions to the board and the replacement of board members is essential. The charge to this committee was to review existing criteria for board membership in the light of the new agency purpose, to set defined periods of board membership and to prepare slates for the election of officers and members-at-large of the Administrative Committee. Unlike other committees to be described, the Nominating Committee was made up solely of members of the board.

For all additional standing or *ad hoc* committees, the president of the board instituted a new pattern. She invited both board and staff members to serve on these committees, and all committee members were to carry equal responsibility for the formulation of recommendations on policies and procedures to be presented to the board for its approval. The concept behind this procedure was that in a nonphilanthropic organization, supported on fees from clients alone, board and staff are engaged in the joint provision of a needed community service. Therefore, the staff has a *collaborative* rather than *participatory* relationship with the board. Most social agencies provide for the responsible participation of staff in the provision of the agency's service. Participation permits the staff to inform and advise the board of the significance for policy formulation of staff experience with clients and staff concerns about personnel practices. Collaboration, on the other hand, requires that board and staff review *jointly* all factors entering into policy decisions, respecting each other's special experience. Respect is best achieved through direct communication, which permits the weighing of the pros and cons of alternatives.

Agencies operating under philanthropic funding assign the role of accountability for use of funds to the board of directors, who are considered to be representative of the donor group. Although professional personnel participate in this accounting by providing data needed by the board, it is the board's role to help raise required funds and account for them. In a nonphilanthropic agency whose income is derived from clients served, it is the practitioner who is accountable to the client for money given in exchange for service.

In reconsidering, then, the role of staff and board in the provision of a service on a nonphilanthropic base, the concept of mutual collaborative responsibility gave rise to the testing out of committees, appointed by the President, whose composition provided the opportunity for joint board and staff thinking and recommendation on all policy matters.

The first such committee appointed was the Research Committee. It was composed of four staff members participating in a research program and three board members. The committee's charge was to determine the role of research at ALCS, to review research proposals, to deal with policy questions arising out of research programs, and to assist in the conduct of these programs when indicated.

The second committee was the Finance Committee, to which were appointed all regular staff members [10] and three members of the board, one of whom was the Treasurer. Its charge was to review periodically the agency's financial status and to recommend policy that would assure the soundness of the fiscal base.

*Ad hoc* committees were similarly established. For example, one committee, consisting of three board members and three staff members, considered a policy for private practice by ALCS staff. A member of the Technical Advisory Committee and of the evening staff were invited to serve as advisors.

With the appointment of these committees, much more direct communication between board and staff was assured. Staff members were also invited by the President to attend all board meetings. At first this was done on a random basis, depending on which staff members were free at the time of a meeting. Later, however, two or three staff members each year accepted responsibility for regular attendance at board meetings. They attended as individuals and not as representatives of the staff, and participated in the discussion of every item on the agenda. They expressed their own opinions, even if these were in contradiction to the recommendations of a committee on which they had served. They did not, however, have a vote at board meetings.

In summary, the founding core of the board initially set the criteria for board member selection and established the term of office and of board membership on the basis that a pilot program is best conducted by an experienced and stable board of directors and group of officers. No changes were made in the board's role or responsibilities at the end of the pilot phase. But as the agency moved toward full funding through fees, there was evidence of uncertainty of their role on the part of board members.

Were they advisory or decision-making? This uncertainty emerged particularly in relation to decisions concerning staff salaries. When the final phase of ALCS was reached, the criteria for board membership were reviewed and sustained. Terms of office and of board membership, however, were limited to specific time periods and a more formal approach to board selection was instituted. Permanent and *ad hoc* committees were appointed but their usual composition was altered in keeping with the concept of an agency in which board and staff are jointly engaged in the provision of a needed community service. Thus committees were appointed by the president to include both board and professional staff members.

## 2. *The Executive Director*

No job description had been prepared for the position of executive director. All candidates for the position were interviewed by four members of the founding group and the board made the final selection. Minutes of board meetings and the Executive Director's recollections of several interviews held with her indicate that the board placed major emphasis on the candidate's interest in the potentials of a pilot program and his ability to conduct such a program. Two criteria were set: substantial and successful experience in social agencies (preferably those offering counseling services), and experience in working with related professions, psychiatry in particular. They foresaw that experimentation would require ability to introduce innovations based on unproven hypotheses and to live through periods of experimentation with the inevitable challenges from within and outside the profession. In their interviews they seemed to be tapping the candidate's ability to foresee the problems of an innovative program and his reactions to dealing with them. Was he overly optimistic or pessimistic? Would he anticipate problems and on what basis? How would he react to challenge, and so forth?

The founders had decided that the service program would be family and individual counseling. But it was left to the Executive Director to recommend how this service would be offered and its relationship to the pilot project. In part the responsibilities of her position were traditional: to give professional form and content to the creation of a service agency. This involved finding appropriate office space, helping design how the space could best be used, developing a program of public interpretation, setting up clerical and statistical procedures, recommending staffing patterns, establishing criteria for the selection of staff, defining job responsibilities, and handling other usual administrative matters. But within even the traditional role, some innovations were possible. For example, in defining job responsibilities, full accountability for the quality of service to clients was to be vested in the practitioner.

While administrative details were one of the Executive Director's responsibilities, her major role was to guide the conduct of the pilot project. More specifically, hers was the *primary* though not sole responsibility for being alert to the effect of innovations on the roles of board, executive and staff. How would, for example, the absence of a philanthropic base affect board-staff roles and their relationship to each other? What was the effect on the executive's role of having only experienced staff? How would the absence of supervision and the vesting of accountability for quality of service in the practitioner affect the service given to clients? A further task was that of isolating the issues requiring either board or staff attention. When was it advisable to call to their attention something inappropriate in their relationship to one another? When was it important to call to their attention client reactions that might indicate need for review of policy or procedure, and so forth?

As a part of her role in guiding a pilot venture, Miss

Fizdale held herself responsible for keeping in touch with professional social workers, both to benefit from their views of the program and to inform them of the progress being made. This was accomplished through meetings with the Technical Advisory Committee, the primary source of exchange with the profession; through meetings with small groups of social workers (educators, medical social workers, et al.) and individual contacts with leaders in the field; through acceptance of invitations to speak before social work groups, nationally and locally, and to offer consultation to agencies on issues related to the work of ALCS. The Executive Director also took on the responsibility to write professional articles, teach seminars, and participate in the work of committees under the aegis of professional organizations when the ALCS experience was relevant to the task of the committee. An example of the latter was continuing participation in various committees of the National Association of Social Workers, which led to the establishment in 1970 of the Certification of Competence Board.

Although she did not define her role as one of direct service to clients, she did carry a few (usually two or three) treatment cases and took all phone calls for initial appointments, whether these were from the potential client, his family or some other source of referral. This latter task was seen as a way of helping her not only to stay related to the experience of direct practice but also to become attuned to the wear and tear of the practitioners' tasks. The intricacies of treatment, the concern one experiences in making difficult decisions, even the problem of scheduling appointments are important to the determination of reasonable production standards. All of these activities served to assist in developing a sounder collaborative role with the staff, particularly in relation to policies on staff productivity.

The decision to take all intake calls was based on several considerations. Certain elements of the project required specific information on the content of the first phone contact. It was necessary, for example, to find an appropriate moment for informing the client of the professional background and qualifications of the staff. Some statistical data also had to be secured. Being less involved in direct practice and more involved in the overall conduct of the program, the Executive Director would be more likely to remember the dual focus of an intake call. The first phone contact also has crucial implications for public relations. The concentration of these calls in one professional person does aid in the development of the skills required. A primary example is the importance in giving the caller a sense of the interviewer's interest in him without establishing a beginning treatment relationship.

This role remained essentially the same throughout the entire life of the agency, equally appropriate in the pilot and final phases of the agency. Both periods called for redesign of structure and conscious awareness of adaptations that would be required. During the interim period some tension was experienced in carrying the total role, undoubtedly because the pilot aims had been achieved and no new goals had been set. In retrospect, during that period Miss Fizdale sensed her role to be one of holding the board and staff to the continuation of a social agency based on support through fees and manned by staff with substantial maturity and experience—characteristics that would have to be maintained if the agency were to become permanent.

### 3. The Casework Staff

The pattern of staffing at ALCS was traditional for family agencies: 1) a casework staff to offer direct services to clients; 2) a consultant staff in psychiatry, psychology and internal medicine, and 3) a clerical staff to handle reception and all clerical processes. The casework staff will be described in some detail because these practitioners were the key to the success of the pilot venture and the prime element in the ALCS structure.

The criteria for the selection of casework staff members and the definition of their roles and responsibilities were initially recommended by the Executive Director to the Board of Directors. The description of responsibilities that follows applies primarily to the "regular staff," who had the dual responsibility for direct practice and collaboration in the conduct of the pilot program and, in the final phase, in the administration of the permanent agency. (The evening or part-time staff [11] were responsible only for direct service to clients, but with the same expectation that they were to carry full accountability for the services given.) The practitioner's full accountability for the quality of his service to clients meant that he would be given no supervision. Consultation (whether from colleagues in the agency or from other professionals) was available when the practitioners desired help in arriving at treatment decisions in specific client situations. He had to take the initiative for using consultation, but he did not have to seek approval in advance, even if consultation added to agency costs. Moreover, consultants, regardless of the profession from which each was drawn, were not responsible for the treatment decisions made. These were solely the responsibility of the practitioner. This meant that when a client was assigned, the practitioner determined whether he would continue with the case or would refer the client elsewhere—to other social agencies or other professional persons. He set his own treatment goals (within the context of the client's consent) and chose the "level" or type of treatment he would offer—educational, advisory, supportive help in dealing with a crisis, or psychotherapy requiring the resolution of intrapsychic conflicts. He decided the "method" or mode to be employed—joint interviews, family or individual interviews, group counseling or therapy—as well as the frequency of interviews. He also determined who, in addition to the initiating client, would need to be involved in all phases of the treatment.

To emphasize the meaning of full responsibility, annual evaluations of performance and a probationary period were eliminated early in the history of the agency. This applied to all staff, whether full-time or part-time. The bulk of the regular staff's work was direct service to clients, but they also collaborated in the pilot project and, later, in the administrative conduct of the agency on a planned and regular basis. Such collaboration involved sharing joint responsibility with the Executive Director in determining recommendations to be made to the board for the design of the project, for policies and procedures essential to achieve pilot aims, and for developing and testing hypotheses and evaluating the results. During the initial and interim phases, they collaborated with the Executive Director in the conduct of the pilot program; in the final phase, they collaborated with the board in administering a permanent agency.

### a. *Criteria for Staff Selection*

The criteria for staff selection were evolved in the six-month period between the appointment of the Executive Director and the opening of the office to clients. About twenty-three candidates had expressed interest. Interviews revealed what each was seeking and why each was interested in ALCS, enabling the testing of certain hypotheses regarding the qualifications and characteristics of the "experienced" staff ALCS was seeking.

In 1954 no criteria had been set by the National Association of Social Workers for the identification of persons able to carry the responsibilities as defined by ALCS, using

the (roughly) descriptive terms then prevalent in the field
in delineating full professional competence: ability to
"practice independently" or "on a self-reliant basis" or
"with consultation only." These terms were subject to
wide interpretation, which varied from agency to agency.
An administrator wishing to establish criteria for persons
who could practice without supervision (or to set up any
new category of caseworker) had to rely on his own experience and judgment or on consultation with peers.

The search for practitioners began with the idea that
the same qualifications and characteristics would be essential for the responsibilities to be carried in the pilot program
and for direct practice with clients, with the exception that
the pilot responsibilities might demand that the practitioner
be genuinely interested in contributing to the development
of the knowledge and skills of his profession. Another assumption involved the vague idea that the mature practitioner had confidence in his capacity to be helpful in a
professional role.

These ideas took more precise form as the Executive Director interviewed the initial group of candidates [12]: the
mature practitioner had a frame of reference from which
he made diagnostic appraisals and treatment decisions.
This might be an accepted theoretical premise, a "school
of thought," or a base representing integration of his training and the practice wisdom he had acquired through experience. The mature practitioner also had an ability to
conceptualize with sufficient clarity to communicate his
thinking to his colleagues. His "school of thought" [13]
was deemed irrelevant to the selection process in view of
the somewhat primitive stage of social work theory at that
time. What was relevant was that he have a consistent base
for his practice and that any variation from his usual
methods represented a deliberate judgment about the needs
of the client. The mature practitioner also had confidence

in his ability to observe and evaluate the effect on his treatment efforts and to make necessary shifts.

Another characteristic sought in the professional candidate was an ability to judge when he needed consultation, from what profession and to answer what questions. The experienced practitioner would not wish to have the course of his future work with clients set for him, but would seek added knowledge to help him set his own goals. He would tend to weigh a consultant's ideas against his own, needing neither to capitulate to others nor to have them agree with him. Generally, he would respond to new theoretical concepts or new treatment methods with a thoughtful appraisal of their appropriate use.

In interviewing, it became evident that not all persons, even with a high degree of competence, can work collaboratively. Collaboration requires a degree of control over normal competitive needs and an ability to focus on the overall objective or on the sound resolution of a professional issue. In addition, it was assumed that staff would have had some experience in dealing with administrative responsibilities if they were to help in the design of a pilot program.

In summary, then, the characteristics needed by ALCS staff were identified as follows:

1)	Evidence of a conceptualized knowledge base for practice.

2)	Confidence in one's ability to observe and evaluate the effect of one's professional intervention upon the client.

3)	Ability to tolerate differences among colleagues in theoretical approaches to practice and to tolerate the inevitable discomfort in an experimental program and the testing of new ideas.

4)	Ability to contribute to innovation.

5)	Interest in the pilot venture and a genuine desire to test out its potential value to the profession of social work.

6)     Ability to work collaboratively with others.
7)     Some knowledge of administrative tasks and processes.

In 1954 persons who possessed these characteristics and had proven competence in direct service to clients were likely to be those in supervisory or senior caseworker positions. At that time persons holding these positions had usually had a minimum of ten years of experience and some supervisory or subadministrative responsibility. ALCS therefore established the requirement of a minimum of ten years' experience with at least one year in a supervisory or administrative position. Preference was given to candidates who had had experience in family or child guidance agencies or mental health settings.

The recommendation that the staff meet these qualifications as set by the Executive Director, was accepted totally by the board, which made no attempt to influence the criteria in any way.

### b.  The Hiring Process

After the first casework practitioner was hired, the entire professional staff participated in the hiring of additional casework personnel. In this process they reaffirmed the qualifications needed for ALCS staff and eventually devised several additional criteria. One of these was that usually the mature practitioner should have a defined career goal. They also believed that personal self-awareness was heightened by an experience in personal therapy, and this criterion was added as a factor of preference. A hiring process was devised consisting of a series of steps over a period of four to six weeks. Its purpose, openly stated to the candidate, was to give him and ALCS an opportunity for the *mutual* and *overt* exploration of their suitability for each other. It was predicated on the belief that the mature and seasoned practitioner does evaluate an agency in which he

is seeking a job. He considers whether he can identify with
the professional values and goals of the agency and whether
the position will further his own career interests. At the
same time, out of a need for continuing self-respect and
pride in his professional performance, he also considers
what he will contribute to the agency. If he has the opportunity to do so, he evaluates his potential colleagues
as professional persons and as persons with whom he can
work in relative harmony. In fact, ALCS believed that *one* of
the indications of a candidate's maturity and competence
would be the extent to which he welcomed the opportunity
for such an open, mutual exploration of interest and suitability.

The first step in the hiring process was a "preapplication"
interview. When an applicant called to inquire about a
position, he was asked whether he met the specific criteria
for length and type of previous experience. If he did he
was invited to the preapplication interview with the Executive Director. It was explained that, because ALCS was
engaged in a pilot venture, some of his responsibilities
would be similar to those he had carried in other agencies
but some would vary considerably. For this reason it was
best if he learned more about the agency before deciding
to apply. No references were secured at this point, even if
the candidate offered them. The content of the preapplication interview was the same for each candidate in any
given period. He was briefed on the history leading to the
establishment of the agency, what its goals were, and the
expectation of eventual termination. His direct service responsibilities were discussed and emphasis was given to the
similarities and differences between the responsibilities in
ALCS and in practitioner positions in other agencies. He
was informed of the personnel practices in effect and how
they had been established. He was also informed of the
steps in the hiring process and it was made clear to him

that the selection of a candidate was dependent upon mutual agreement among all staff members, including the
Executive Director.

All these factors were elaborated in the preapplication
interview to help the candidate consider how each factor
might affect him if he were invited to join the staff and
chose to do so. To illustrate, let us take the factor of the
life-expectancy of the agency. During the pilot years (and
even into the interim period) the candidate was told about
the five-to-ten-year life-expectancy of the agency. This was
an important consideration for everyone, but especially for
the older candidate, particularly before the agency provided a retirement program. After 1961, candidates were
informed that the agency would continue as long as the
need for it existed and as long as it could be supported on
fees alone. The philosophic premise behind this planning
was explained and each candidate was urged to consider
whether he could identify with it since it would be an important factor in his future satisfaction in the agency. This
was often a difficult point for candidates to understand,
but it became clearer when we discussed how increments
in salary were decided in other social agencies in contrast
to ALCS. To achieve salary increments at ALCS, the staff
had to determine how ALCS would secure the necessary
funds. The pros and cons of various alternatives for securing funds would be reviewed by the staff and a joint decision would be presented for board approval (prior to
1965). In the final phase, the candidate would be informed
of the collaborative process of board and staff in the fiscal
management of the agency.

The candidate's responses to the full discussion of the
special characteristics of ALCS provided insight into his
sense of his professional competence and interest in the
project. Often the project intrigued him. In fact, it was
sometimes necessary to warn a candidate not to be carried

away by the "charismatic" nature of the project but to consider its appropriateness for him at this stage in his professional career. His responses also gave clues to his reactions to innovation and whether he could anticipate what his reactions would be. Could he live through the testing of new ideas? Could he appraise the agency (its practice, values and goals) realistically in the light of his own interests and career needs? Could he anticipate his reactions to the fact that his conceptual base of practice might be different from that of his colleagues?

At the conclusion of this interview, the candidate was given an application form. He was encouraged not to fill it out immediately but to think about the interview and to call if he had additional questions. If he decided to apply, his return of the form would signal his interest in ALCS taking the next step.

References were secured after the application was returned. During the pilot years, usually a summary of their content and implications was provided to the staff. Later, however, the staff reviewed all references prior to meeting to determine whether ALCS should encourage the applicant to continue. When it was decided to do so but there was some question relating to a reference, another interview was arranged. If there were no such questions, the applicant was invited to examine any aspect of the agency he wanted to understand in greater detail. His request was the base for what was made available to him.

Some candidates were interested in reading records as examples of various client requests and how current staff members handled them. Record reading gave the applicant some indication of the nature of treatment responsibilities he might have to undertake as well as what he might gain from peer exchange and consultation. A selection of records was always available to a candidate. Some candidates were interested in statistical data because they had difficulty in understanding how a practice was built and the length of time required to build it. Others asked about the consultation available or wanted to read minutes of staff meetings or seminar discussions. After a candidate had read the material, he was offered the opportunity to discuss his reactions with the Executive Director. In this exchange, more was learned about his knowledge base, his evaluation of himself in relation to treatment responsibilities as revealed by client requests, and his tolerance for differences and for nonconformity in treatment policies. It also provided some perspective on his knowledge of and tolerance for administrative processes. A report of this interview was made to the staff at the subsequent staff meeting.

The next step in the hiring process was the candidate's meeting with the staff as a whole, usually by attending a staff meeting or a seminar session. He would be briefed so that he could participate in the discussion, and encouraged to come to the meeting ready to make his own evaluation of the staff as future colleagues, as he had doubtless already evaluated the Executive Director. He was asked to consider what he could gain from such an association and what he could contribute to the group. Would he anticipate having any problems in working with the group? He understood that the staff would be making the same kind of evaluation of him. After this meeting, he could again meet with the Executive Director to raise any questions he might have; he could also meet with other members of the staff.

Questions were frequently raised by candidates in meeting with Miss Fizdale. For example, was one or another of the staff members the accepted leader? Was a particular staff member always so competitive? To what extent did the ideas of one staff member, forcefully expressed, influence the practice of others? Direct answers were given to such questions, but attention was called to the concern evidenced in the question as something he ought to consider as he made his decision about working in the agency. Would the competitiveness of a staff member make it difficult for him to participate soundly in group discussions? How would opinions forcefully expressed affect him? Why was he concerned about the possibility of a particular staff member's being the accepted leader? The candidate was usually discouraged from revealing his initial reactions to these questions which he needed to answer to himself. The staff also reviewed their reactions to the candidate in a later group meeting.

The final step involved asking the candidate to make available to ALCS one or two examples of his current practice. [14] These records were read independently by all members of the staff. Reviewing records of a candidate's practice was perhaps the most important factor in our final decision. Many articulate people can create an excellent impression in discussion, but a review of their practice recording can uncover gaps between theoretical knowledge and its use, as well as their capacity to observe client reactions and to understand messages that are conveyed indirectly. The reverse also occurred: the less articulate candidate's competence was more apparent in his records than in group interchange. Reading the case material helped focus impressions gained in interviews with the candidate, in participation in meetings, and through references, providing a clearer picture of his practice skills and his suitability for the responsibilities he would have to carry. In the staff meeting to consider the candidate, the case material was weighed in relation to the other impressions in coming to a final decision. The assets he could bring to the group process were summarized, and some of the problems he might have in the setting were explored. Should ALCS suggest that he consider these possible areas of difficulty before accepting the invitation to join staff? What were the indications that he would not meet the requirements of the

position? The group decision was then reported to the
applicant, usually in an interview with the Executive Director. During this interview the applicant often raised some
final questions, and the details regarding his coming were
completed. If the candidate had come through to this point
in the hiring process and it was decided not to invite him,
he was also offered an interview to discuss the basis of the
group decision. [15]

As previously stated, the content of the various steps
changed as the program of the agency shifted from that of
a pilot attempt to reach a target clientele to that of a continuing service for the clientele ALCS had reached. The
method of selection did not change.

### c. Avenues of Staff Communication

There were two weekly staff meetings, the first of which,
called the administrative meeting, was chaired by the Ex-
exutive Director and lasted for two hours. In the director's
absence, a staff member, selected on a rotating basis, took
the chair. At the administrative meeting, recommendations
for policies and procedures were formulated, qualifications
of candidates for positions were reviewed, and significant
trends observed in the new client group were discussed.
During the pilot phase, this was also the meeting at which
staff took part in peer group consultations on cases and reported innovations they were undertaking. Discussions also
concerned what the staff were experiencing and observing
about themselves in the process of adjusting to the new
roles and responsibilities carried at ALCS, particularly complete accountability for quality of service, and developing
recommendations for board action on policies and procedures. During the interim phase, the meetings continued
to deal with these administrative matters, but peer consultations were more likely to be held in small groups. The
meetings then began to take on some elements of the

mutual exploration of professional problems in which the consultant in psychiatry seemed to have no particular role. In the final phase of the agency, the administrative meeting increasingly served as a channel for group exchange concerning treatment innovations and studies initiated by staff members. It also promoted adjustment to the emerging concept of staff members as equal partners and collaborators with the board in providing some needed community service. Administrative matters not requiring board participation or action were also discussed at this meeting. Those matters that involved joint action were reviewed by the appropriate agency committee.

The second weekly staff meeting was the psychiatric consultation meeting. At first it was three hours in length and was led by the consultant in psychiatry, with all staff attending. Since ALCS had started with no defined in-service training program, this meeting took on some of the characteristics of an educational seminar. At times policy issues were discussed, particularly as they pertained to the treatment of clients or the need for additional consultants. [16] Eventually, the case consultation, which had been the original focus, was held separately. Staff found that individual case consultations were the most fruitful. One hour was then set aside for this purpose and the group meeting was reduced to two hours in length. It became primarily educational and eventually served as the focus for the evolution of a group program of additional learning defined by staff and based upon their felt lacks in knowledge and skills that interfered with the fulfillment of their responsibility for quality of service to clients. In the final phase of the agency, the psychiatric meeting was used entirely for seminars that were conducted by a consultant hired for this purpose. The staff determined the seminar content.

### 4. *The Consultant Staff*

The Executive Director took the responsibility of selecting the first consultant and of establishing the criteria to be met by any consultant subsequently engaged: substantial experience and competence in his professional discipline, high regard by his professional colleagues, and substantial knowledge of the aims and practice of social agencies. Staff collaborated in defining the qualifications and the role of additional consultants, as the need for them became clear. Persons who met the necessary qualifications usually were suggested by our first consultant. However, staff also knew of qualified persons and, at times, leaders in the field of psychiatry were consulted for suggestions. [17] There were three regular consultants, one in psychiatry, one in psychology, and one in internal medicine. The board played no part in choosing the consultants, but they were informed of the criteria set.

The consultants' responsibilities in ALCS were the same as they are in other settings: consultation to staff on specific treatment problems; keeping staff abreast of pertinent developments in their own professions. It was clearly understood that they would not carry any responsibility in regard to the treatment decisions made on behalf of a client, with the exception of the client who was potentially suicidal or homicidal. Eventually the consultant role was extended to the giving of seminars, and the consultant in psychiatry offered each staff member a period of regular consultation to help him acquire increased skill in psychotherapy. The content of seminars and the focus of individualized consultation were determined by the staff.

The consultants did not attend board meetings except by invitation, the Executive Director serving as the primary channel of communication between them, the board and the Technical Advisory Committee.

The staff were also free to seek consultation from persons

who were not our regular consultants [18] but who met our established criteria. This they could do without administrative clearance. The practitioner made the decision, selected the consultant and merely informed me that a bill for consultation on a specific client would be forthcoming.

## 5. The Clerical Staff

All clerical staff were involved in client reception, regarded as the most important part of their responsibility. They were the first to greet clients, whether over the phone or in person, although they did not make intake appointments. [19] They did, however, check the client's name against a master card index so that a previous record could be given to the Director or to the professional discussing with the client his request for an appointment. The receptionist also collected fees from clients according to the agreement reached between the client and his practitioner (whether after each interview or by monthly billing). Clerical staff were responsible for informing the practitioner of any unusual, possibly significant behavior of the client while he was awaiting his appointment or of any deviation in the pattern of payment that had been agreed upon. In addition, they processed statistical data, typed and kept records and performed all clerical duties, including billing.

The qualifications to be met by a clerical staff member were a college education and interest in assuming a paraprofessional function, since his responsibilities would expose him to many unexpected client reactions and would require him to exercise considerable judgment in dealing with them. He would have to be clear about his own role and its relationship to both the treatment and the pilot programs. Minimal clerical competence (typing, filing, ability to learn a switchboard) was also required but was considered secondary.

The Office Manager screened clerical applicants for clerical skills and for evidence of ability to learn; the Executive Director then interviewed qualified candidates to assess their probable responses to unexpected situations, their judgment and their ingenuity. The actual hiring was done by the Office Manager. Staff and board were informed of the criteria but did not participate in setting them or in hiring clerical personnel. [20]

The Executive Director was the main channel of communication between the clerical staff and the professional staff or board. At first the Office Manager attended all casework administrative meetings, but this practice was discontinued because she felt that it was not sufficiently productive to warrant the time given. Occasional meetings between the professional staff and the Office Manager were arranged as requested by either. During the pilot phase, monthly staff meetings were held with the clerical staff in order to keep them related to the overall program of the agency and to increase their skill in dealing appropriately with clients who presented unusual problems for them. Eventually this function was taken over by the Office Manager who, when she deemed them advisable, then arranged for meetings with the Executive Director. She also served as secretary to the Executive Director and attended all board meetings.

### 6. *The Technical Advisory Committee*

Many leading social workers had been consulted by the founding group as they were discussing the potential value and design of the pilot program. The board favored the appointment of a Technical Advisory Committee, leaving the decision to have such a committee and the membership criteria to the Executive Director. Because they could bring pertinent experience to the development of the client service program as well as the design of the pilot program and eventual evaluation, leaders from voluntary family agencies were asked to serve. Five executive directors of New York City's family agencies and the executive director of the Family Service Association of America became the core of the Technical Advisory Committee. Each was selected because he was a leader in the field of social welfare as well as an executive. He was encouraged, however, to bring with him to committee meetings persons from his own staff whose counsel he would need in responding to the questions posed. At various times during the pilot phase, the advisory committee members brought public relations consultants, budget directors, research specialists and leading supervisory personnel.

The function of the Technical Advisory Committee was to help ALCS achieve the goal of providing the profession with information regarding the target clientele to the end that the profession's future relationship with and responsibility for this client group could be defined. The committee was expected to participate in designing the project with respect to setting the policy on fees, giving advice on the criteria for selection of staff and consultants, setting the questions to be answered by the pilot program, and so forth. Members were also asked to assess the significance of ALCS experience as it evolved and to offer counsel on what else ALCS needed to do to increase the value to the profession of the information acquired. Their advice was also sought on professional questions not specifically pertinent to the pilot program. For example, they were consulted about the policy on referral of waiting list clients to private practitioners and about the length of time records should be kept after treatment was completed. Their primary role, however, was to help ALCS make its pilot program useful to the profession and to help evaluate the significance of its experience.

Meetings of the Technical Advisory Committee were called when needed and committee members would consult individually with the Executive Director between meetings. The Executive Director served as chairman of the committee. [21]   The board President attended all meetings and occasionally other members of the board were present. Joint meetings of the board and the Technical Advisory Committee did not take place during the pilot phase; but during the interim and final phases of the agency, some were held so that the board could hear directly the committee's ideas on plans affecting the future direction of ALCS.

The composition of the Technical Advisory Committee changed as persons who had been executives of the five agencies moved into other professional activity, but they remained as members because they had been invited as leaders in the profession. Others were added who were executives of agencies or who had other responsibilities which would enable them to contribute to the achievement of the ALCS pilot aims. The executive director of the National Association of Social Workers was asked to serve because of his broad knowledge of the concerns and interests of social workers, and his acknowledged leadership in the field. A number of ALCS innovations were directly pertinent to the work of special committees of NASW, and his participation helped assure an interchange of ideas between ALCS and NASW committees.

The role of the Technical Advisory Committee was never redefined, but the committee met more frequently and was consulted more often during the pilot program and toward the end of the interim phase. At this latter point, the committee began the process of evaluating the pilot program and issued a report to the Board of Directors in 1963. Although the report did not so state, the members clearly favored the continuance of ALCS as a service agency for the middle- and upper-income groups in New York City and its environs. They were invited to remain as consultants to the permanent agency that was being formed, although one member raised questons about the validity of having such a committee in a permanent agency. He believed that a more appropriate channel of communication would be an organization such as the Family Service Association of America. [22] This matter was still under consideration when the program of client service was transferred to the newly formed Park East Counseling Group in 1969. The Technical Advisory Committee's connection with the client service program ended in January, 1970. Members agreed to be on call in an advisory capacity in the completion of the residual pilot responsibilities: the disposition of records, the use of unspent funds, and the issuing of reports to the profession. It was anticipated that these responsibilities would be completed by January, 1972.

This completes the examination of the administrative structure evolved by ALCS and the changes that took place during the life of the agency. Though described separately, the functions, roles and responsibilities of each component part—board, Executive Director, casework staff, consultant staff, clerical staff, and Technical Advisory Committee—were interrelated. In some ways, each component unit had consciously to make adjustments to a total structure that demanded new attitudes and new views of the mission of a nonphilanthropic, innovative social agency.

# 2. *Policies and Procedures*

LIKE THE development of the administrative structure, the establishment of policies and procedures was an evolutionary process. To show the continuing interaction of the component units of ALCS in this process and how the client group affected policy decisions, the account will be developed chronologically.

## Type of Service

It will be recalled that the founders conceived of ALCS as a family service agency, but one which would offer only one service—casework counseling. They thought that focusing the public's attention on casework counseling was more likely to emphasize the professional character of social work than if ALCS also offered services of a more tangible nature. The advance publicity stated that ALCS would offer counseling for problems of marital or premarital discord, disturbed relationships among siblings or between children and parents, concerns about the development of children, the effect of physical or psychological illness of one member of the family on the lives of the others, as well as help with individual problems such as vocational or educational underachievement, and failure to develop meaningful peer relationships. The ALCS role was defined as "helping with the everyday problems" of families and individuals. The descriptions of the service, like those of other social agencies, reflected a desire to encourage families and individuals to seek preventive help and to distinguish social work's professional competence and roles from those of several related professions offering similar services. [23]

No restrictive policy was established relating to who (within the specified economic bracketing) would be served or how they would be served, with the exception that potentially suicidal or homicidal clients and those whose physical condition (e.g., hypertension, bleeding ulcers) might be aggravated by the treatment of emotional problems would be referred to a psychiatrist. This policy remained essentially the same throughout, although it was subsequently reformulated more forthrightly and realistically. In the reformulation, the fact was taken into account that it is not always possible to identify severe acting out tendencies in the early stages of treatment and, moreover, that referral to a psychiatrist, because of its meaning of rejection or hopelessness to some clients, sometimes increases the risks of his acting out. Therefore, the revised policy stated that in such instances, referral to a psychiatrist was a preferred policy, but that the practitioner would be allowed to exercise judgment in deciding on such referral. When referral was contraindicated, safeguards existed in the use of ALCS consultants in medicine and psychiatry.

The most significant factor in determining whom ALCS would serve and with what type of service resided in the staff themselves. In hiring practitioners and by every means possible thereafter, emphasis was placed on their freedom and responsibility for making such determinations. In reviewing a client's situation, each staff member was to be guided by his diagnostic appraisal and the consequent treatment needs of his client, as well as by his self-appraisal of his competence to offer the help required. He had complete freedom and responsibility to serve the client when he was confident he could do so, without regard to how his colleagues might decide if the client were theirs.

This policy resulted in the staff's engaging in careful self-appraisal, often becoming involved in identifying gaps in their knowledge and in seeking remedies for their lack. The practitioners decided what training program they needed, including outside seminars independently taken at first, which were later added to seminars in the agency. They also undertook some experimentation or innovation in treatment, but within a framework of careful study and review. [24]   As their competence grew, the range of their counseling services expanded to include psychotherapy when the intrapsychic problems of the client prevented growth or change in his patterns of response to others and his ability to cope satisfactorily with his life situations and tasks.

ALCS did not offer other services these clients required, such as housing for the aged or for post-hospitalized patients, special education programs for children, and temporary care of children. These were available to the target clientele through other private services, the most notable of which was Adult Counselors and Home Finders, manned by two experienced social workers. [25]   This agency was able to help ALCS clients secure a variety of concrete services, taking into account the personality and individual needs of the person and his family. Policy regarding the type of service to be offered was developed by the staff. The board and the Technical Advisory Committee were kept informed of expansion of traditional services.

## Fees and Fee Policies

A fee had to be established before beginning to serve the client group. The founders, it will be recalled, had been interested in determining whether the target clientele would pay a "substantial" fee for casework counseling. But it had not been decided what "substantial" meant in actual dollars or how the fee was to be determined. In the six months between engaging the Executive Director and opening ALCS to clients—and indeed even earlier when the founders were exploring their idea—a number of formal and informal consultations on this question were held with individual leaders in the fields of medicine (psychiatrists, internists and pediatricians primarily), law, psychology, and social work. [26] Some of them advised setting a modest fee as a precaution against negative reactions from professionals in related fields, who might see ALCS (caseworkers) as intruding into their domain (psychologists, psychiatrists, et al.). Others advised high fees as a means of interesting the target group, the premise being that the middle- and upper-income person tends to equate quality of service with its cost; a high fee is more likely to imply a high caliber of service. A few advised that the fee be related to actual cost, recognizing, however, that this might be difficult to ascertain.

The policy adopted by the board fixed the interview fee at its actual cost. All costs, including those for personnel, maintenance, office operation, and public relations were to be allocated to the unit of service—the interview. The board agreed with staff recommendation that, to reflect the nonphilanthropic nature of ALCS, the fee would have to be identical for all clients. This policy remained unchanged throughout the life of the agency, but the items to be included in the cost accounting of the fee changed with experience.

Three factors enter into costing an interview and therefore into the determination of a full-cost fee: the actual costs (housing, staffing, consultation, public interpretation, general overhead); staff productivity (the number of interviews practitioners carry and the size of staff considered optimal for the agency's purpose); and fee collection (what loss in anticipated income will occur because of waived or unpaid bills). In computing the fee only those costs deemed essential to the service program were included. Costs incurred solely as a result of the pilot aims were not included in the computation of the fee. Allocation of costs to service or pilot program was determined by the Treasurer in conference with the Executive Director and was approved by the board. The bookkeeping system carried separate entries for pilot costs and service costs. For example, costs of studies undertaken by staff to improve services to a specific client or group of clients were included as service costs and were used in computing fees. But the cost of research undertaken to increase the body of professional knowledge was not included.

What ALCS actually spent for client service was governed by two factors: the demands of a high caliber service (for example, the salaries required to attract the professional personnel defined as essential); and the nonphilanthropic character of the agency. For example, it was agreed that consultants would receive their regular fees and that it was necessary to build a contingency fund. The standard of production (always determined by professional staff) included a minimum expectation of the number of interviews to be conducted by each practitioner, consistent with the definition of "without detriment to service." [27] Costing also included determination of the optimum staff size.

The first fee established in 1954 was arbitrary, however, pending the accumulation of experience with costs, staff production and client payment. It was set at $10.00 an interview—an amount less than the $15.00 fee generally charged by psychiatrists in 1954, but considerably higher than the fee usually charged at that time by other social agencies in New York City. [28] In setting the fee, the length of the interview was not discussed by the board. Shortly after the service began, the staff informed the board that individual interviews would be forty-five minutes and

family or joint interviews would be sixty minutes. [29]  For
no recorded reason, the same fee was established for each
kind of interview. Later, higher fees were set for joint and
family interviews and for interviews held outside of the
office (home visits, school visits, etc.). The fee for each
participant in group counseling sessions was set on the expectation of there being eight to ten people per group. Although *in toto* it brought more money into the agency, the
rate per client was less than for individual interviews. Computation of these fees included normal costs as well as
anticipated extra costs: travel time for visits; additional
consultation required; extra equipment needed for group
therapy. The fee for individual interviews remained the
same throughout the initial 1954-57 period.

Just as the fee was initially established arbitrarily, so was
the level of expected productivity. Staff informed the
board that a minimum expectation of five interviews per
worker per day would be tested. With experience, however,
5.4 interviews per day were found to be the consistent interview productivity of all staff during the pilot years. In
computing production, it was agreed, based on the staff
experience that each new staff member needed from three
to six months in which to build a practice of sufficient size
to produce this number of interviews. [30]  It was also
found that the original concept of an optimal staff of four
or five for the pilot project had to be revised to meet the
demands of the case consultation process. A staff of seven
to eight was found to offer more likelihood of a large
variety of staff experience, and hence of ideas that could
enrich discussions and consultations. A group of ten or
more was found to introduce other problems, the primary
one being difficulty in keeping discussions focused on the
questions raised by the practitioner requesting consultation.
When case consultation was removed from the administrative staff meeting, a group of seven to eight was still

considered the optimum for the development of policy recommendations and for professional discussions.

Experience also showed that the anticipated loss of income—twenty percent—from unpaid fees was far too high; in the pilot years, considerably less than one percent of fees was unpaid.

When the fee was reconsidered in 1958 (the end of the pilot phase), the consultant in fiscal management estimated the cost of an interview on the basis of an expected minimum production of 5.4 interviews per worker per day with a staff of seven. He took into account the decisions made concerning cost items to be covered in computing the service fee and our experience with unpaid bills. He then computed the fee by dividing the total anticipated costs of the service program by the anticipated number of interviews to be held. The basis of the new fee, which had been discussed with the staff, was then reviewed by the Treasurer, who presented the supporting data for the new fee first to the Administrative Committee and then to the board for final review and action. The new fee was set at $12.50 for an individual interview and $15.00 for a joint or family interview. The same process was followed two years later when the fees were again increased to $15.00 and $20.00 respectively.

In 1966, a new process of fee-setting was introduced. The consultant in fiscal matters presented his recommendations and supporting data, and the pros and cons of various alternatives directly (without prior clearance with anyone) to the Finance Committee (which now was composed of three board members and all regular staff). [31] The committee then reviewed the data simultaneously and made a recommendation which was presented to the board by the Treasurer, as official chairman of the Finance Committee, for review and action. The need for an increase in staff salaries was a vital factor in the final decision. The new fee was set

at $17.50 for an individual interview and $25.00 for a joint
or family interview. The committee had recommended that
no salary increase go into effect until six months had
elapsed, pending experience with the amount of additional
income produced. Salaries were then increased in July, 1966.
The same fee revision process was followed in 1969, except
that the goal set was a $20,000-a-year base salary for regu-
lar, full-time staff.

With each fee increase, beginning in 1958, a decision had
to be made concerning its applicability to the current client
group. Each time, the staff recommended that the fee be
the same for all clients—new, reapplying, or current. But
in 1958, the board decided that the new fee would apply
only to new and reapplying clients because they believed
that ALCS had entered an implied contractual agreement
with the current clientele to offer treatment at a specified
cost and should not abrogate the contract. Consequently, it
was three years before all clients were paying the same fee.
In 1960 the board asked staff to inform their current clients
that the new fee would affect them in six months, to allow
a reasonable period in which clients could complete treatment or find a resource at a lower fee elsewhere, if they
wished. In 1966, however, when board and staff, as joint
members of the Finance Committee, considered this policy
question, it was agreed that the new fee would apply immediately to all clients—new, currently served, or reapplying.

Consideration of economic hardship for the client,
whether occasioned by a change in his life situation, such
as severe cut in salary, or by a new fee, was always an integral part of the practitioner's role as therapist. It is interesting to note that clients who were in treatment in 1958
and 1960, who were not affected by an increase in the fee,
thought our action was a considerate gesture. When a few
clients objected to the fee increase in 1966, their reactions

were reviewed and appropriate action was taken. The old fee was continued, at least for the time being, when there would be hardship for the client (one situation) or when an increase was contraindicated because of specific therapeutic reasons (one situation).

Both board and staff believed that, consistent with the nonphilanthropic character of the agency, all fees should be paid. Staff also considered fee payment essential for therapeutic reasons since the client's pattern of payment could well be related to the problems which brought him for help. They assumed that dealing with the problems of fee payment was inherent in the treatment process and, therefore, was the practitioner's responsibility. When they considered it essential for therapeutic reasons to collect a delinquent bill, they made every effort to do so. On occasion they found that they could not be effective. The practitioner always had two options. He could decide to waive a fee and send a memo to this effect to the clerical and administrative staff. No administrative clearance for his decision was required. The Administrative Committee of the board was informed in writing of all waivers. When the practitioner decided that a bill should be collected, his second option was to let the client know that failure to complete payment by a certain date would mean that the bill would be submitted to the "Business Committee" of the board for their decision on further action. (In actuality, the business committee and the Administrative Committee were the same.) Later, at the staff's suggestion, a lawyer was retained and some bills were referred to him for collection. The client was informed that this would be done. When a referral to the lawyer was made, the practitioner sent him a memo with such information as would help him deal with fee collection intelligently. It did not contain details of the person's history or problems. The general policy, in which the lawyer concurred, was that he would carry out whatever steps were necessary up to but not including court action. In view of the minor problem of unpaid bills and the insignificant sum of money involved, the need for this step was questioned by a member of the board who had carried this legal role for a time. Nevertheless, it was decided to retain a lawyer because staff saw this as an essential step in the therapeutic process in some instances.

In 1954 the staff set a policy that clients would be charged for all broken appointments and those not cancelled twenty-four hours in advance—a policy common to other fee-charging social agencies. This policy was easier to enunciate than to administer, however. Many of the cancellations made at least twenty-four hours in advance were the result of client reactions that needed to be recognized in the therapeutic process itself. On the other hand, clients taken suddenly ill resented being charged for broken appointments. Since it was not possible to use the time assigned to these appointments for other income-producing interviews, the policy was changed. Clients were informed that fees would be charged for *all* appointments not kept. Clients who called to cancel were offered another appointment if a mutually suitable time could be found *within a week* and charges were made for appointments that could not be shifted. Clients were informed of these policies when it was agreed that they would be coming in regularly and time was being reserved for them. No payment was required for an appointment cancelled by the practitioner or for broken or cancelled *intake* appointments. In the rare instances where a client repeatedly broke or cancelled an intake appointment, an effort was made to help him face his ambivalence, whatever its cause; the client was assured that the agency wished to avoid charging for unkept initial appointments. In a few situations when the client called the practitioner directly for a new appointment and kept breaking it, because a relationship had been established, a bill was sent. Both the

board and the Technical Advisory Committee were kept
informed of the practice.

*Case Records and Recording*
Whether case records of treatment were essential was considered several times over the years, beginning with the
first staff appointment and the first client interview. What
purpose would the record serve in a nonphilanthropic
agency made up of experienced practitioners in whom
accountability for quality of service was vested? Any recording done for research purposes would be dependent
upon the requirements of the research. Was a record of the
client's past problems and treatment needed in the event he
reapplied for help? Supposedly the client's report of the
"facts" of his past and certainly their significance to him
could change if therapeutic help has been effective. His
current concepts, not his changed view, are at the base of
diagnosis. Yet the fact that change has occurred can be
diagnostically significant. The value of process recording
was also questioned on the basis that it did not truly reflect
what had occurred and that it fostered the worker's feeling
that he had to justify his decisions to someone else, rather
than promoting self-appraisal.

Each time the issue of keeping records was raised, the
staff reaffirmed their conviction that recording is essential
for sound service to clients. The values identified included
the following: the *process* of recording provides a structure
for review of one's diagnostic appraisals and assessment of
the intervention planned or undertaken; such appraisals
are constantly thought about by the practitioner as he
serves his clients, but putting his thoughts on paper forces
him to sift his clinical observations and cull what is essential
for making treatment decisions. The written statement then
becomes a base for future evaluation of one's service and
for testing the validity of one's previous appraisals if the

client reapplies. The staff also believed that a client would expect an *agency* to maintain some record of his contact, so that if he returned (or chose to go elsewhere) and his former practitioner were no longer with the agency, he would not need to repeat information he had already given. [32]

Defining the *content* of the record was not easy. Many staff meetings were devoted to the subject and staff committees studied it intensively. Members of the Technical Advisory Committee were also consulted. It was finally decided that two types of records were needed: an agency record and a worker's record.

The *permanent agency record* for all clients, regardless of the length of contact, was a 5″ x 8″ card, kept in a central file. This record was dictated at the point of case closing. If contact consisted of one to six interviews, this card was the *only* record. If, however, it was anticipated that treatment would require long-term contact, a temporary folder record was also kept. Both records covered the same information, but more detail was recorded in the folder record, including dictated summaries of the first six weeks of contact and of changes that occurred over varying periods of time.

The 5″ x 8″ card recorded the following: the client's request (how he viewed his problem), the precipitating factors in his seeking help, the practitioner's view of the client's problem (diagnostic evaluation, impressions), the treatment objectives, the extent to which these objectives had been achieved, the reason for closing, whether the reason was similarly perceived by worker and client, and the practitioner's assessment of the client's future need for help. The folder record contained in the first summary the same data regarding the client's view of his problem, but added whatever shifts had occurred in his perception in the first six weeks. It also covered precipitating factors, diagnostic appraisals (or questions and impressions), immediate and potential treatment objectives, and the client's defense mechanisms. Pertinent historical data could be included but were optional. The periodic additions to the folder record dealt with changes in each of these categories of information. The agency records (card or folder) were kept in a central file. The folder record was retained for five years following the termination of treatment and then was destroyed. The 5″ x 8″ card was kept.

Neither of these two kinds of agency record met the practitioner's needs in his continuing work with clients. Each practitioner felt he had to keep notes as a method for recalling important data and the detail of the treatment process. At first these notes were dictated but it was found that professionals tended to consider dictating as a method of informing another person rather than as an aid to one's own work. So it was soon agreed that each worker would keep whatever longhand notes he wished and in whatever form was best for him. Some workers kept separate notebooks for each client; others had one looseleaf notebook divided into sections for each client or wrote notes on loose sheets and inserted them in the folder record. Some staff members made notes during the interview, others directly after. Some jotted down only sentences of significance or words that served as a pivot of recall. Others made what appeared to be an outline of the process of the interview.

Each staff member had a locked file in his office in which all his notes were kept. The Executive Director made no attempt to ascertain that notes were actually being kept. [33] But obviously all staff members did keep them, judging by the fact that workers were always ready to produce illustrative material for seminar discussions. For example, one seminar dealt with the manifest content of dreams and their use in psychotherapy. Each staff member at one point or another was asked to report the content of a client's dreams over a period of months. Since all staff were able to do so, even in cases begun before the seminar was held, it can be assumed that full notes had been kept. At the point of case closing, the worker could decide what he wanted to do with his notes. As a rule, they were not useful for other practitioners because of the problem of legibility and of the "codes" used, which had meaning only to the person who wrote them. Some practitioners chose to place their notes in the agency folder; others retained them separately, and some destroyed them.

The staff also set the policy on currency in dictation. They decided that for long-term cases, an *intake summary* covering the content described above was to be dictated within six weeks from the initial contact, and a folder record was to be set up. No backlog on dictation of these initial summaries could be accumulated because the major value in this dictation was its assistance to the practitioner in clarifying diagnosis, possible treatment objectives. Thus it had value for treatment of the client. Periodic additions to this record would be made before the worker's vacation at the very least, but could be made at other times.

The value of the *closing summary* lay in its usefulness to the practitioner in self-appraisal, but it also served certain administrative purposes. (It had less value to the treatment of the client.) Keeping closing dictation current facilitated the accumulation of information about client requests, which had a bearing on program planning. It made possible the economical use of clerical time as well as the ready review of information concerning the target clientele being reached. So it was decided that a backlog of closing dictation could not be accrued for longer than six months. Two deadlines for closing were agreed upon—December 30 and May 30.

When these decisions about currency of dictation were not fully carried out, the staff were asked to review the policy. They eventually agreed that the policy needed some "teeth": If a practitioner failed to meet the deadlines for either opening summaries or closings, he would not offer intake appointments to clerical staff until the backlog was cleared up. The rationale for this decision was that the practitioner who did not meet the deadlines set was unable to sustain the expected caliber of service and therefore his practice should be reduced, with the attendant loss in income for "extra" interviews. [34]

The board, as always, was informed of all experimentation and decisions regarding record-keeping. While board members asked pertinent questions, they made no attempt to make decisions in this matter, which they regarded as wholly a professional prerogative. But the Technical Advisory Committee was consulted as staff ideas developed about the content of records and the length of time they should be retained. They offered advice and were interested in observing staff experience.

### Affiliate Program and the Waiting List

By the winter of 1957, ALCS had acquired a sizeable but meaningless waiting list. Potential clients were not inclined to wait for appointments. It was as if they could not conceive of being unable to find someone to serve them since they could pay a fee. They often asked for suggestions of other resources for help, such as social agencies and private practitioners. [35] They appreciated the offer to call them as soon as an appointment was available and responded warmly when called to inquire if they still wanted to come. When there was a delay of even one week, it was obvious that the client had gone to another resource or his motivation for help had diminished. (Only a few waited. These were usually people who had been advised to see a particular practitioner.) When staff could ask what source of help had been reached, it often appeared that the client's choice had been accidental and that he had few guidelines concerning the qualifications to be sought in persons engaged in family or individual counseling.

The board was concerned about this report of ALCS experience—at one point (during 1957) asking why these persons were not referred to casework practitioners in private practice. Private practice was then still a controversial issue, with no definite stand having been taken by NASW and no professional regulation of such practice. Accepting responsibility for referral to caseworkers in private practice would have involved ALCS in a time-consuming, costly project of creating a list of qualified persons, at the same time placing the agency in the midst of an unresolved professional issue. The board accepted the recommendation that staff consult with the Technical Advisory Committee before establishing a policy.

The Technical Advisory Committee considered the matter but saw the problem of referral to private practitioners as affecting all agencies and requiring a formal stand on the part of NASW. This meant not only deciding whether private practice was possible within the profession of social work but also setting standards for such practice and regulating it, or else informing the public clearly that the private practice of social work was not possible. The committee agreed to join the staff in urging NASW to take action, and in exploring some possible interim plan for the agency to meet its responsibility to those who called for help but who could not be served as clients.

A series of meetings was set up to which were invited several leading caseworkers in private practice, the Executive Director and Associate Director of NASW, members of the ALCS board and members of the Technical Advisory Committee. [36]   In these meetings it was apparent that everyone was concerned with the lack of standards for private practice and the lack of regulation. The private practitioners also discussed the effect on them of being outside the mainstream of the profession. They believed that the knowledge they had acquired in private practice had important implications for the training and supervision of practitioners in philanthropic settings, and the lack of their acceptance within the profession created problems in their efforts to secure other needed services for their clients—services which were available only through social agencies.

An outcome of these discussions was the plan adopted by ALCS for an experimental program entitled "Affiliate Staff." [37] This program provided for a contractual agreement between private practitioners and ALCS. The agreement was designed to deal with the concerns of the profession about unregulated private practice, to reduce the isolation of the private practitioner, and to provide an avenue of exchange between private and agency practitioners. Although the affiliate program was to be carried out by ALCS, it was written with the idea of its potential use by other social agencies. One of the agreements in the contract was that ALCS would refer to its affiliate staff members those clients who could afford the ALCS fee but for whom an appointment could not be offered. Affiliates were to be persons who had been former members of the ALCS staff. One staff member left to go into private practice in 1958 and entered into an affiliate agreement with ALCS to test the plan. Clients on the agency waiting list were referred to her. The program was viewed as an interim measure pending action by NASW concerning private practice. Although it became inactive as a formalized arrangement in 1962, referrals to former staff members continued. [38]

## Public Interpretation Program

The ALCS public interpretation program began officially with a series of personal interviews with leaders in private education, medicine, law, and the clergy. A fact sheet [39] stating ALCS objectives in some detail was sent to persons selected by members of the board, with a letter asking them to grant an interview to the Executive Director. The ALCS public relations consultant also joined in the interview. The purpose of each visit was to describe the agency to someone who was in a position to make referrals; to ask how he thought ALCS services should be offered to the target clientele; and to gain his ideas on how best to inform others in his profession of the new resource.

These interviews strengthened the initial intent to place more emphasis on developing sources of referral than on appealing directly to potential clients. Announcing ALCS services through a newspaper advertisement had been discussed, but had been decided against because paid advertisements might detract from the agency's professional stance, particularly since all professions tend to avoid any semblance of commercialism. Some newspapers did give coverage to the opening of the office. These reports were dignified, emphasizing the ALCS intent to reach a clientele who could pay "full-cost" fees, and letting the public know that ALCS professional services were similar to those of other social agencies.

Between 1954 and 1959 a program of direct approach to potential sources of referral was maintained, largely through personal contact and a series of "open house" afternoons. Some of these sessions were planned for lay leaders invited by members of the board. Others were for groups of social workers, physicians, and psychiatrists invited by the professional staff and consultants. [40] A brief explanation of the ALCS program was made; the group was urged to ask questions. Judging from the referrals made after these meetings, the open house format was highly successful. Invitations were also solicited to speak before professional groups, primarily social workers but also lawyers, clergy, and school faculties, and to present the program to boards of directors of other agencies. Informal person-to-person talks with headmasters, clergy, and others were also productive. Not only did they result in some referrals, but they also gave insight into the difficulties such persons face when they consider referring a family or individual for counseling.

ALCS criteria for staff selection, the quality of its consultants, and the fact that the Technical Advisory Committee represented various professional "schools of thought," were all conducive to the establishment of trust in the agency's intent to serve the profession as well as clients. The outstanding quality of its board served similarly to establish trust in ALCS among lay leaders and sources of referral.

After 1959, no consistent program of publicity was carried out although occasional notices appeared in the press from information provided freelance writers and reporters on a specific subject they were researching. Beyond that, planned publicity was confined to announcements of new staff, giving their educational and professional qualifications. A letter including this content was sent to everyone who had made a referral. Similarly, new brochures and announcements of an increase in fees were sent to all agencies and individuals who had referred clients to ALCS.

Although there was frequent discussion of the need for additional publicity, two factors seemed to have inhibited action: the unclear future of the agency between 1959 and 1962; the concentration on designing a permanent agency model. There was also need to delineate an interpretive program addressed specifically to the client group for whom the service was intended. Though ALCS had reached a middle- and upper-income group, it was believed that more such persons would use the service if they could be informed of it. The agency's consultants recommended that staff write articles for magazines and newspapers read by those in the upper-income group. [41] Such media as *Wall*

*Street Journal, Vogue* and *Barrons* were suggested. Had the agency continued, someone equipped to write for these outlets would doubtless have been sought.

One formal report was issued in 1958, again setting forth aims, achievements to date, and the aims to be pursued in the future. [42]

## Conditions of Employment and Personnel Practices

Only two conditions of employment had been set before the agency opened its doors to clients: a salary of $6,000 per year for all practitioners and a 37½-hour work week. Thus the first practitioner, who arrived on June 28, 1954, and the Executive Director had the task of evolving recommendations for the board on all other conditions of employment, including personnel practices.

Information was gathered on personnel policies in several major New York City agencies. It was believed that some of the personnel practices that were usual to other social agencies had to be adopted by ALCS to assure the agency's competitive position in securing staff. Others were set conditionally, to allow time to gain experience. The President of the board urged basing recommendations, insofar as possible, on the expectation of hiring only experienced and mature staff. For such people, personnel practices could be flexible because one could rely on their integrity in achieving the purpose of the program and on their professional responsibility to clients.

Recommendations were presented first to the Administrative Committee, which then presented them to the board for final action or for their information. Having staff gather the information on personnel practices in comparable agencies, consider the applicability of such practices to an agency headed toward self-support through fees, and evolve a policy for board action was a new procedure. In most social agencies, these are responsibilities of a board committee.

But ALCS philosophy dictated that the staff should be thus involved in accordance with their responsibility for the pilot program design.

This procedure proved to be viable, *except in the area of salary decisions.* In 1954 the board approved the Executive Director's original salary recommendations. But from 1955 on the board altered them, with the result that considerable tension was experienced by staff, executive and board in arriving at an acceptable base for policy formulation on salaries. After the Finance Committee was set up in 1965, it assessed all proposals regarding policies on the conditions of employment, since almost every change in personnel practices and in conditions of employment (with the exception of probation and evaluations) is tied to finances in some way. Therefore, the Finance Committee carried a major role in formulating all such policies. When considered jointly by members of the Finance Committee within the context of the agency's fiscal needs if continuity were to be assured, the amount of the salary was agreed upon and guidelines for future decisions were established. The strain was thereby eliminated.

### 1. *Vacations* [43]

Supervisory and senior casework staff in the major agencies in New York City usually had five weeks of paid vacation in 1954. Because this was a highly prized practice, it was recommended for ALCS staff, and the board approved. After 1961, however, a practitioner could arrange for additional vacation time if he had met his annual interview production standard in less than the 246-day work year. [44] There also had to be adequate coverage for his practice and no anticipated adverse effects on clients.

Initially the staff proposed that vacations be scheduled between June 30 and September 15, allowing for the option of reserving one week for the Christmas and New Year holidays. The recommendation was based on the expectation that clients would be vacationing at the same time and the demand for service would therefore be less than at other times of the year. Experience soon revealed that there was no predictable period in which client requests for service were fewer than at other times. The summer vacation period then extended until October 1 and spring vacations could be arranged if one's practice could be covered adequately. The board had known of our initial policy and was informed that the change had been made on the basis of experience.

### 2. Legal Holidays

The staff recommended in 1954 that the office be closed on the six universally observed legal holidays: New Year's Day, Memorial Day, Fourth of July, Labor Day, Thanksgiving and Christmas. No plan for observing other legal holidays was proposed until experience had tested this policy and what could be afforded financially. The board did not approve Memorial Day as a legal holiday comparable to the others suggested. However, since it was found that clients did observe that day, the office was closed in 1955 without prior board approval. The number of legal holidays on which the office was closed never increased, even though the agency could have afforded the extra cost. Clients often wanted appointments on other legal holidays, even when these were being observed in their own places of employment. Moreover, staff members were free to take extra days off so long as they maintained the minimum interview production expected.

### 3. Religious Holidays

It was proposed initially that five days a year be allowed staff who wanted to observe religious holidays. At the time the effect this policy might have on agency income had not yet been fully realized. When production norms were set (five per day; later, 5.4), it was assumed that a worker's annual interview production would be reduced by five (or 5.4) interviews for each day of religious observance. The policy was approved and remained in effect until 1966, when the attention of the Finance Committee was called by one of the group to an inequity in it. Those who observed a religious holiday were credited for extra interviews on the basis of a lower annual interview expectation than those who did not. The Finance Committee considered various alternatives, but decided not to lower the production expectation for those who observed religious holidays. In effect, this eliminated the provision for paid religious holidays. Those who wished to observe a religious holiday could use their vacation time, could make up the loss in production, or could choose to receive less additional income earned through "extra" interviews. The board was told of this change. [45]

### 4. Personal Leave

Requests for personal leave were granted in accordance with the reason for the leave. [46] This policy remained unchanged. Production expectations of professional staff for the year were reduced according to the number of days taken.

### 5. Sick Leave [47]

The policy on sick leave was the one that most reflected confidence in a mature practitioner's sense of responsibility. No minimum or maximum amount of sick leave allowance was set. Rather, a practitioner who was ill was to receive his normal base salary throughout his illness, in the expectation that most illnesses would be brief. If he had a serious illness requiring a lengthy absence from work, the period of continued salary coverage was to be determined on an individual basis. It was assumed that in such an event the practitioner would make plans for other financial coverage of his needs which ALCS would help him realize.

The costs of what were seen as "normal" periods of illness were covered in fee computation by an allowance of an average of five days of illness per year per practitioner. This computation was based on a staff of seven persons. The abnormal or long-term coverage cost, to be decided on an individual basis, was seen in 1954 as being supplied by the overall foundation grant. When the agency moved toward permanence on a self-support basis, the policy was reviewed by the Finance Committee and sustained. It was agreed, however, that the cost of the policy could not be wholly supplied through the contingency fund which was established in 1961 and added to each year thereafter. This was particularly relevant if two or more staff members were ill at the same time. [48] It was then recommended that the agency purchase maximum income protection insurance for each practitioner to insure continuance of a portion of base salary for a period of five years. The contingency fund could then supplement this insurance in accordance with the person's length of service at ALCS, up to a maximum of one year. Premium costs for income protection insurance were added to administrative costs and were then included in the computation of the fee.

### 6. Insurances

The first practitioner and the Executive Director assumed that ALCS would offer staff the insurances offered by other social agencies—Blue Cross, Blue Shield or Group Health Insurance, and Workmen's Compensation. Retirement insurance was not recommended initially, primarily because the agency's lifetime expectation was a maximum of ten years. But in 1958 a retirement insurance program was instituted, purchased from the National Health and Welfare Retirement Association. The recommendation that this be done came from a member of the board, who was concerned about the loss of several excellent candidates who could not afford to accept positions because no retirement program was available.

The need for some insurance against unexpected drains on income (low intake, sudden reverses in the financial capacity of the client in treatment, prolonged illness of a staff member, and so forth) was apparent once the decision was made that the agency become permanent and self-supporting. In 1961 the Treasurer conceived of the establishment of a contingency fund, which was approved by the board, and part of the excess income in fiscal 1960-61 was placed in it. The staff were not consulted regarding its establishment. [49] Though they made no formal objection, they did raise questions about diverting into the fund earned income that could have been used to increase their salaries. But when the agency structure was reorganized and they were appointed as members of the Finance Committee, they came to see that the contingency fund was a form of salary insurance as well as insurance that the agency would continue to be a resource for clients.

The Finance Committee was also concerned about other potential drains on income and whether the contingency fund would be adequate. They recommended in 1968 that malpractice insurance be taken out for the agency and individual staff members. The additional expenses of all insurances, as well as of the contingency fund, were carried as administrative expenses, included in fee computation.

## 7. *Production*

An early problem for the Executive Director and the first practitioner in setting the design of the agency was how many interviews a day an experienced practitioner could carry without detriment to service. Included in the definition of "without detriment to service" was the time required for all activities connected with meeting a client's needs—consultations, telephone calls, dictation, reviewing one's practice to observe trends with specific clients—and sufficient energy to be alert in interviews and to participate fully in staff meetings. Workers would have no responsibility for training of students, engaging in community activities, or gathering statistical data. [50] Although some activities affecting productivity, such as recording, had yet to be defined, it was anticipated that a production rate of five interviews a day within a work week of 37½ hours should present no problem. Therefore, the board was informed that this production expectation would be tested and reported to them as the staff gained further experience. During the pilot years (1954-57), the staff maintained a minimum of 5.4 interviews a day, with some practitioners exceeding this amount. [51] This then became the base number on which all interview costs were computed after 1958.

During the interim period it also was apparent that despite variation from practitioner to practitioner and from year to year, all practitioners held a minimum of 200 extra interviews a year. In 1969, therefore, when the Finance Committee was considering how a base salary of $20,000 a year could be achieved, the 200 extra interviews were added to the minimum expectation of production, making a yearly total of 1,410 interviews instead of 1,210. The base salary was then set at $20,000 a year.

## 8. Work Week

A work week of 37½ hours, usual in social agencies, was established. The office was open from 12:30 p.m. to 9:00 p.m. on Monday and from 9:00 a.m. to 5:30 p.m. on all other weekdays. From the beginning, however, emphasis was not placed on the hours a practitioner was physically present in the office, but on the fulfillment of his responsibilities. It was assumed that mature practitioners would meet their responsibilities and that it was not necessary to keep a check on when they came or went. They were expected, however, to inform the receptionist of their schedules and where they might be reached in the event of an emergency.

In time the work week of each practitioner became exceedingly flexible, in response to the individual needs of specific clients. Not all clients could come in on Monday evenings. Others, requiring evening appointments, needed more than one appointment a week. When it became apparent that treatment of clients required flexible scheduling, arrangements were made for the office to have reception and clerical services available from 9:00 a.m. to 9:00 p.m. Mondays through Thursdays. Staff could then schedule appointments more flexibly. (The office closed at 5:00 on Fridays.) A few practitioners did see clients on Saturday mornings, but the number was small and no clerical coverage was planned. The work week had been the initial base of decisions regarding production. However, the 37½ hours became unimportant in the light of the wish to be more available to clients.

### 9. Probation
In hiring the first worker, no mention had been made of a policy concerning a probationary period, on the assumption that this was inconsistent with the demands of a pilot program. New workers in the early years reacted as if they were indeed on probation, and after 1956 each candidate was told that there was no probationary period since it was not consistent with the transfer to the practitioner of full accountability for the quality of his practice. [52]

### 10. Evaluations
No system of periodic administrative evaluation of staff

was established: to have done so would have been inconsistent with the concept of a team of equals, or a partnership, which underlay the pilot program. It would also have
been contrary to the hypothesized desired relationship between client and practitioner in the interest of a high caliber
of service. [53]   When the board was informed of this
policy, many members concurred because they had long
questioned the value of evaluations for professional personnel. Others asked questions, but all concurred that the
decision was one for the professionals to make.

### 11. Resignations

The first worker and the Executive Director made no
recommendation concerning a policy on resignations; it
was believed that the traditional month's notice would be
sufficient. [54]   But later experience with clients forced
a review of this "no-policy." Within the first year it was
noted that clients reacted unfavorably to being shifted
from one practitioner to another. This was first obvious
in relation to having the intake evaluation made by one
practitioner and the client transferred for continued service to another practitioner. There was no justifiable reason
for this procedure except when the client had to be transferred for therapeutic reasons. Consequently, a new policy
was adopted to have the worker continue with the clients
assigned to him at the point of intake (unless transfer was
indicated for therapeutic reasons).

The full impact of client response to transfer was not
felt until the first staff resignation occurred. The worker
reported that, to her surprise, a large proportion of her
clients were refusing to be transferred to another practitioner despite their recognition that they needed additional
help. This experience was in such direct contradiction to
what the staff had had in other agencies that it was agreed
to observe whether the same problem arose when the next

worker left. One was scheduled to leave within a few months. Before the effective date of her resignation, the staff as a whole reviewed her practice load, identified those clients who needed to have additional help, and suggested how to deal with their potential reactions to transfer. Despite this, the first experience was repeated: a number of clients who recognized their need for additional help nevertheless refused to be transferred.

This observation led to the hypothesis that clients who pay the full cost of counseling service feel free to give direct expression to a need experienced by all clients—a need for continuity in service from the practitioner who has been helpful to them. It appeared that this expectation is valid and that failure to provide continuity (within the limits of life situations) can be a disservice to clients. To assure continuity, however, the policy regarding resignations had to be reformulated.

Thus in 1958 ALCS established the policy that a practitioner who resigned could leave his full-time position whenever his administrative tasks were completed. But he would be required to continue as a part-time employee for the purpose of completing treatment of those clients for whom transfer would be therapeutically unsound. Again, this was a policy formulated by staff, after consultation with the Technical Advisory Committee, and considered to be in the realm of professional decision-making. The board were informed of the policy and its rationale. The policy was amended in 1959, concomitantly with the formulation of policy concerning referral of waiting-list clients to caseworkers in private practice. In the latter instance, it was decided that clients could be referred to former ALCS staff members who were in private practice and who maintained an affiliate relationship with ALCS. [55] Therefore, the person who resigned from ALCS could elect either to remain as a part-time employee or take the same clients into his private practice so long as he retained an affiliate relationship with ALCS.

In 1966 the requirement of retaining an affiliate relationship was removed because the affiliate program was discontinued. A regular staff member who resigned could then arrange to see his former ALCS clients on a private basis. In considering this policy, the effect of a staff member's resignation on the financial status of the agency was reviewed. The Finance Committee recommended that a regular staff member (going into private practice) give six months' notice of his intent to resign. During this time no new clients would be assigned to him and he would be paid according to the number of interviews held.

The policies on resignation applied only to regular staff; part-time or evening staff were expected to complete responsibility to clients as employees of ALCS. They were hired with the understanding that they would resign only after treatment of their assigned clients had been completed. All policies on resignation were reviewed by the Technical Advisory Committee which agreed that practitioners must have an ethical means of continuing treatment of those clients for whom a transfer would be a disservice. The Technical Advisory Committee had also considered whether an unethical person might use his position with ALCS as a step toward building a private practice, but concluded that no policy could deal with such an event. Although the Board of Directors recognized the financial impact of the policy on ALCS, they believed that six months' notice was sufficient for securing a staff replacement and that client needs had to take priority over the agency's financial interests.

### 12. Salaries

The Executive Director's recommendation in 1954 that all staff receive the same salary ($6,000 a year, which represented the top of the salary range for similar personnel in New York City social agencies) actually contained two policy proposals. The first was that staff of equal competence and approximately equal length of experience, carrying the same roles and responsibilities, should be paid the same salary regardless of the length of time they had worked in the agency. The second was that ALCS salaries remain competitive with those in other New York City social agencies for comparable personnel. The board approved the recommendation as sound for an experimental venture.

It was harder to implement the policy of equal pay for equal responsibility than it was to gain initial board concurrence. Within the first year, the board decided to give a "merit increase" to the first practitioner on her anniversary date in June, 1955. They labeled it a "merit increase" so that there would be no assumption that anniversary raises were to be automatically given to all staff members. The board did not respond to the Executive Director's expressed concern that the resulting differential in salary could be detrimental to the desired team relationship of peers for the conduct of the pilot program. The staff (then consisting of four practitioners) agreed that the board's decision would upset the design of the pilot program. Rather than challenging the board's authority, it was agreed that there was a need to "educate" the board further and at an "appropriate moment" to attempt to restore the policy of equal salaries.

In November of that year, the board voted a salary increase in a similar fashion to the Executive Director, whose reaction was extremely negative. What was intended as a gesture of approval and confidence forced her to consider why she reacted so unfavorably. [56] As a result, she was able to confer with the president of the board concerning the inappropriateness of the board's action in *both* salary decisions, pointing out that nothing had been added to the knowledge necessary for determining guidelines for salary decisions in a potentially self-supporting agency. In such a pilot demonstration, the professional staff would have to consider what guidelines on salary should be recommended to the profession and to social agencies that wanted to develop their own self-supporting units. The president of the board agreed but advised that staff salaries be equalized on anniversary dates by giving the other three practitioners the same salary increment of $300.00 which had been given to the first practitioner and so inform the board. The policy of equal salary was thus kept loosely in effect but was not restored by official board approval until 1957. By that time certain characteristics of a group practice had begun to emerge at ALCS and the board were interested in it as a potential model for the future delivery of service to the target clientele. Since professionals in group practice generally received equal salaries, the board reaffirmed their desire to foster the concept of a group practice by maintaining equal salaries for ALCS practitioners.

In accepting the initial recommendation for the *actual* salary, the board had assumed that staff salaries would always be similarly determined, namely to keep ALCS competitive with other New York City social agencies for comparable personnel. In fact, the board had asked the Executive Director to inform staff that their salaries would increase as salaries for comparable staff in other social agencies increased. By contrast, the Executive Director had assumed that the competitive guideline was temporary, to meet the needs of the moment in helping ALCS secure staff in the beginning, and that how salaries would be determined in a self-supporting agency would be one of the matters for the professional staff and Executive Director to consider as the pilot program developed. While the Executive Director had several ideas concerning future guidelines, such as the possibility of salaries being tied to production, she believed firmly that a desirable solution could evolve only from experience.

Staff initially appeared satisfied with the periodic raises the board voted them during the pilot years ($7,000 in 1957 and $7,500 in January, 1958), perhaps because they saw these as fair for a pilot project of short duration. They were receiving the top salary then paid in social agencies. They certainly involved themselves vitally in arriving at decisions affecting fees and the agency's ability to achieve self-support. Staff set the norms for production, for essential recording, clerical coverage, and so forth. Yet when the agency became increasingly supported by fees, they merely expressed dissatisfaction with their income; they did not become involved in seeking ways to fund salary increases, but seemed to revert to thinking of this as a problem for the board to solve. They regarded the Executive Director's attempts to involve them as not made in good faith but as a way of keeping them from getting increases, despite open discussion of their questions. [57] Yet they did respond to the solution that the Executive Director suggested in 1958 for securing additional income: Since all of them were holding more than the five interviews a day upon which the self-support fee computations were made, why should they not receive extra compensation for their additional interviews? [58] This was presented to the board and approved so that after 1958 the staff received a base salary and additional compensation for each interview above the minimum, computed on a monthly basis.

In 1959 the staff expressed its belief that a base salary of $10,000 a year would be consistent with their level of experience and competence. The Executive Director reported this to the Administrative Committee, which then asked that the two Treasurers, the consultant in fiscal management and the Executive Director meet with staff to see whether this goal was possible. As a result of this meeting, the board agreed to the Treasurers' recommendation that staff salaries be raised to $8,000 a year for a production of 5.4 interviews per day (or 1,210 per year). They would continue to receive compensation for extra interviews. The board decided that the staff's goal of $10,000 annual base salary could not be considered until there were seven staff practitioners. The staff had recommended that income anticipated from the then two unfilled positions be replaced by the use of money granted by the Lehman Foundation, but this proposal was rejected by the Treasurers and the board. At this time, however, another principle was enunciated by the board: whenever the agency incurred a surplus, some of it might be apportioned among regular staff members.

In 1961, when ALCS had its first surplus, the Treasurer recommended and the board approved, without prior discussion with the staff, that forty percent of the surplus be divided among the regular staff (sixty percent going to the building of a contingency fund). From 1961 through fiscal 1965, this policy was followed, with money distributed among staff as a year-end salary adjustment. The decision regarding the amount was always made by the board on recommendation by the Treasurer.

The staff reacted unfavorably to year-end adjustments. The money was welcome, but their exclusion from the process of decision-making was not in keeping with their concept of themselves as professionals as much identified with the goal of agency self-support as were the board members, and certainly responsible for the achievement of this goal. Staff took no action, however, nor did they request a review of the practice. [59]

During the interim period and until the formation of the Finance Committee in 1965, the staff's opinion was that their salaries should be comparable to those of caseworkers in private practice. It was with private practice that the agency was competitive for staff. The board contended that the staff did indeed earn as much as persons in private practice if they took into consideration the things that ALCS provided which private practitioners had to buy on their own.[60]   In fact, the only point of agreement between board and staff was that the Executive Director should be able to make each side see the logic of the other's point of view. Facts concerning the income of private practitioners were difficult to obtain. Although an effort was made to do so, it was not pursued, perhaps because the Executive Director did not believe that facts would really resolve the difference among board, staff and herself. She believed it would be essential to develop some means of *direct and consistent* communication between board and staff so that they might experience the mutuality of their objectives and responsibilities. However, the type of communication channel established would be crucial. To bring board and staff together *solely* for the purpose of discussing salaries would be to invite "negotiation." It would not necessarily create the atmosphere of mutual goals and mutual problems to be resolved. In a number of meetings, the President of the board and the Executive Director discussed how to aid the two groups in seeing that their objectives were the same and how to encourage joint consideration of factors involved in achieving their aims. When the agency was set up on a permanent basis, it was agreed to test a preconceived design for shared decision-making by having the President appoint both board and staff members to serve on all committees.

The Finance Committee was established in 1965. [61] Despite some initial problems of readjustment in their traditional relationship to one another, members of this committee were able to achieve a unity of approach. It is interesting to note that in the minutes of a meeting of the

board discussing a Finance Committee recommendation in
January, 1966, the following statement appears:

> Since [ALCS] salaries are not dependent upon
> philanthropic contributions but upon the earnings
> of staff through fees, the board's view cannot be
> the same as in traditional agencies. It would seem,
> therefore, that the board and staff would need to
> arrive at an educated guess as to what fees are like-
> ly to be possible for their client group and to relate
> salary to this.

The guideline for salary determination then seemed to
have shifted from one of being competitive with other
social agencies to one geared to the productivity of an
experienced staff within the requirements of sound practice and limited by the "marketplace."[62]

In July, 1966, the base salary was advanced to $12,500.
Biweekly checks were issued for base salary and monthly
checks for compensation earned through extra interviews.
Year-end adjustments of salary were discontinued.[63]  In
1969, the base salary was increased to $20,000, with the
increase in minimum production expectation to 1,410
interviews a year. Simultaneously, it was agreed that compensation for more than 1,410 interviews was to be computed at the end of each year and covered by one annual
check.

### 13.  Private Practice for ALCS Staff

The issue of whether ALCS practitioners should engage
in private practice did not arise until 1958 when an applicant who had a small private practice and a goal of entering
such practice on a full-time basis asked whether he would
be permitted to retain his private practice. He was hired
with the understanding that he could continue his private

practice, but would not use his ALCS connection to build that practice.[64]   Later that year, a second person was hired on the same basis. When the board was informed, no objections were raised. But this policy was changed on board initiative in 1960 and without staff consultation. Two prior policy decisions (no limitation on extra interviews held by staff; amended policy regarding the resignation of staff entering private practice [65] ) were responsible for this reversal. The board saw these policies as providing adequate opportunity for staff members to increase their income and providing fairly for those leaving the agency to enter private practice, since they were permitted to keep some clients until treatment was terminated. Exceptions to the "no private practice" policy were permitted only for the two staff members already engaged in it. New staff appointed after 1960 were informed that they could not engage in private practice and of the reasons for this policy.

The new policy and its exceptions did not create a problem as long as ALCS was a temporary agency. However, after 1962 and the establishment of ALCS as a permanent agency, all policies and procedures had to be reviewed, and a policy covering private practice was obviously a priority matter. An *ad hoc* committee consisting of two members of the board and two members of the regular staff, with a member of the Technical Advisory Committee and one of the part-time staff as consultants was appointed. It recommended that the individual practitioner be considered autonomous in deciding whether to engage in private practice and what form it would take (teaching, consultation to agencies, or direct service to clients).[66] When the board reviewed the committee's recommendation, it took the untraditional step of voting to ask that the *entire staff* review the committee's proposals and the board's discussion of it, and carry responsibility for the final decision. Although the board feared that such a policy could create conflict for the practitioner between his responsibility as a participant in a group practice and his interest in private practice, it believed that staff should be responsible for the final decision.[67] The staff did review the board's questions and comments but voted in favor of accepting the *ad hoc* committee's recommendation. As indicated above, this policy formulation in 1967 clarified responsibility for production to maintain the agency on a self-supporting basis, as well as the policy regarding resignation of staff entering into private practice.

This chapter has devoted considerable detail to the way ALCS policies and procedures were developed in order to highlight how respective roles and responsibilities of component units of social agency administrative structure change when the agency's source of income changes and when the agency has a staff ready for full professional role and accountability. Hopefully, it is obvious by now that ALCS evolved new relationships among and between the various units in the agency structure and that professional staff carried policy formulation responsibility different from and beyond that of their counterparts in more traditional settings. The detail recorded here perhaps will have another value in emphasizing that the new roles and responsibilities of professional staff created the need for readjustment for them, board and executive. This will be developed further in another section. Attention is being called here to the areas where readjustment for all created no obvious strain and was easy to achieve, and to the areas where real strain and problems existed, requiring alteration of agency structure in its channels of communication. Since many agencies are concerned with devising new alignments between laymen and professional personnel to achieve their mutual goals of providing service, a review of the ALCS experience may facilitate their own processes.

# 3. *Were the Aims of ALCS Achieved?*

AS WE NOTED earlier, a research program was contemplated from the beginning, to gather statistical data and information designed to answer the various anticipated questions of the profession and to test the hypotheses concerning the target clientele and the objectives. It was not difficult to determine the statistical data needed to identify the client group reached. Competent researchers with necessary experience for this purpose were available. But the real problem was how to gather other information, particularly where the direct involvement of the client group was necessary and could pose treatment complications. Even a relatively simple study of why clients chose ALCS rather than another social agency would not necessarily be viewed by the client as an integral part of his purpose in coming to the agency. Avoiding unnecessary obstacles to treatment or even securing only superficial information required that the research design be constructed by a person knowledgeable about counseling as well as well as research. There were few such persons in 1954 and they were in great demand by many agencies. Moreover, they usually had a primary sphere of interest and were more likely to be willing to work for an agency whose interests coincided with their own.[68]   Since none was readily available, ALCS began with a research consultant who set

up a statistical system to gather data that would emerge
naturally in the flow of content during treatment interviews.

Some of the conclusions that follow are validated statis-
tically; others must be viewed as conclusions drawn from
observation and experience of sufficient weight to warrant
reporting. [69]   Before opening the doors to clients, the
Executive Director formulated a series of questions in
consultation with members of the Technical Advisory
Committee, a few other leaders in the field of social welfare, and members of the Board of Directors. These questions, it was agreed, must be answered if the program were
to be helpful to other communities interested in designing
similar programs.

### Whom Did ALCS Reach?

To define the client group reached and determine
whether they were indeed a "new" client group, data were
sought regarding the education, vocation and income of
the clients as well as what sources of help they had used
previously.

*ALCS clients were generally a well-educated group.* With
few exceptions, they had at least graduated from high
school—never less than 94 percent in any year. An average
of more than 40 percent had completed college, and about
20 percent had done graduate work. The percentage of
those who had completed college dropped over the years
from a high of 80 percent to 41.6 percent, but the reasons
for this are not readily apparent. The percentage of referrals from social agencies had not increased nor had the
number of clients who had previously sought the services
of a social agency; therefore, ALCS was not picking up the
waiting lists of other social agencies. The drop may reflect
the agency's lack, after 1959, of a consistent program of
interpretation designed specifically to reach its target
clientele. [70]

ALCS clients were heavily concentrated vocationally in the professional and highly technical occupations (40 percent). [71]   Another 35 to 40 percent held executive positions, as managers, officials or owners of businesses. [72]   Unskilled workers never exceeded 3 percent of ALCS clients. A major philanthropic agency in New York City, which made its unpublished data available to ALCS, stated that 27 percent of its clients came from the professional and technical groups, in contrast to an average of 75 percent of ALCS clients.

*ALCS clients in the main were economically advantaged.* [73]   The median annual income in the fiscal years l966-67 to 1968-69 ranged from $16,602 in 1966 and $19,695 in 1969. [74]   For the same years, the median income of clients of the major voluntary agency mentioned above ranged from $6,500 to $7,540. The median income of white families in New York City in 1968 was $9,623. [75]   In l966, 49.1% and in 1969, one-half to 70.2% of ALCS clients had annual incomes between $15,000 and $35,000+, in contrast to the clients of the voluntary agency mentioned, where 4 to 8 percent had incomes of $15,000 or more and only a few of these were above $20,000. [76]   The percentage of ALCS clients with incomes ranging between $35,000 and above $200,000 was small, ranging in the 1962-1969 period from zero percent in 1962 to 8.1 percent in 1964. No comparable figure is available concerning voluntary agency clients.

Although social agencies were a major source of client referral, *only a small percentage of ALCS clients had previously sought help from a social agency,* never more than 17 to 18 percent in the earliest years and not more than 10 percent in the last years. [77]   On the other hand, *more than one-third of the clients had had previous psychiatric treatment.* (This group does not include clients who had also sought social agency help.) This proportion remained stable in the last ten years. Therefore, one can conjecture that a sizeable portion of the client group had had problems before applying to ALCS and had sought the help of psychiatry rather than of social work. It is also important to note that more than half had never sought help from any source—social agencies, medical clinics, psychiatrists or nonmedical therapists. Obviously there is a large middle- and upper-income group which would use social agencies if their services were given in a manner comparable to the way in which other professional services are provided. These facts led ALCS and its Technical Advisory Committee to conclude that ALCS had indeed reached its target clientele.

### Why Did They Choose ALCS?

The question then was: *Why had ALCS been able to attract them and serve them?* Certain assumptions regarding the expectations of the target client group had been made in setting up the agency: that they would expect experienced practitioners, a fee fixed and publicized, and a pleasant, professional setting. No survey was conducted to verify the extent to which any of these factors accounted for clients' selection of ALCS, but some evidence indicates that these assumptions were valid. At the time of arranging the initial appointment, the client was usually asked how he happened to learn about ALCS. Though this question elicited information concerning the source of referral, it also provided reasons for his having chosen the agency. Many clients had come because they had heard that ALCS staff consisted solely of experienced practitioners. Some, who had been referred by other social agencies, commented on the ALCS method of fee-setting, stating that they preferred to be told the fee in advance rather than have it set in an interview. They did not see the relevance of questions regarding their income, since they were prepared to pay the fee requested.

Other factors also entered into their choice. Some came because *they trusted the person who referred them:* a physician, a lawyer, a former client of ALCS, a social worker friend, and so forth. Others came because they knew of no other resource, wanted to avoid a long waiting list, or had confidence in a service whose standards were attested to by lay community leaders. Some stated a preference for treatment through a group practice, which they thought would be of higher quality service than that available from a private practitioner. And some chose ALCS in preference to seeking help from a psychiatrist because of a number of preconceived ideas or prejudices: psychiatrists never confine their help to dealing with a client's crisis; they prefer analytic cases; they involve the person in long-term treatment because such practice is easier than short-term treatment and also more lucrative. It is difficult to know how many of these clients would have gone to any social agency had they been referred.

The reasons referring persons gave for their choice of ALCS were also of interest. Physicians, for example, were inclined to send their middle- and upper-income patients to ALCS because they saw its procedures as consistent with "private practice." The set fee and the quality of the staff were important to them, as was the policy of honoring a request to assign the client to a specific counselor. Social workers who referred friends and family members chose ALCS primarily because the staff was experienced, but the promptness of service was also a factor. Frequently the referrer assumed that there was a relationship between the quality of service and the size of fee or said that the potential client would assume that this was so. In our society a common assumption is that the higher the fee the more likely is the quality of service to be high, too.

Unforeseen client expectations included continuity of service from the same practitioner and immediate service.

These clients generally did not accept the need to wait for an initial appointment.

In conjunction with the Technical Advisory Committee, the conclusion was reached that the three factors hypothesized as influential in the client's choice of ALCS were indeed important: a set fee based on costs, an experienced practitioner, and pleasant surroundings. The Technical Advisory Committee saw these factors as facilitating the use of social agency services. To these can now be added the expectation of immediate service, of continuous service from the practitioner to whom the client is first assigned, and of assignment to a specific counselor when requested.

## What Help Did They Request?

The next major area of questions set for exploration in the pilot program concerned the kinds of help the client requested and needed. Were the requests similar to those made of family agencies? Were there any additional requests? [78]

Since three-fourths of ALCS clients were married, it is not surprising that from 40 to 50 percent of the requests (averaging 47.2 percent over 15½ years) were for marital counseling. The next largest number of requests (20 to 25 percent, averaging 23.3 percent) were for help with problems in relationships between parents and children. These requests were related primarily to children living at home or still financially dependent upon their parents, but they also included adult married children and their parents in which emotional separation had not been sufficiently achieved. The remainder of the requests were varied and included help with other types of family relationships (e.g., among siblings, concern for the elderly), but were heavily weighted toward assistance with personal problems: premarital problems, difficulty in establishing meaningful relationships with peers, inability to make vocational choices, and educational or vocational underachievement. There were also requests for help in finding special resources for the aged, the ill, the temporary care of children, or the so-called "concrete" social services.

To meet these requests, ALCS used the range of casework services common to family agencies in general. These included placing at a client's disposal information about community resources or knowledge derived from professional training and experience, as for example, age-appropriate behavior of children; aid in the resolution of a problem involving difficult choice alternatives; help over an immediate crisis; assistance in the resolution of intrapsychic conflicts that inhibit growth or change in patterns of response to others or in coping with usual life tasks. During the early ALCS years, the latter clients were usually referred to a psychiatrist, reasoning that the skills required were "outside the scope of social work competence." However, some clients would not accept the referral and would either come back to ALCS or would not go anywhere else. In reviewing these situations with the consultant in psychiatry, it became obligatory to clarify what was meant by "outside the scope of social work competence." That phrase, it became evident, actually identified lacks in social work's preparation of future practitioners for psychotherapeutic counseling, and the staff then moved to acquire the knowledge essential for this kind of service. Referrals to psychiatrists did decrease as the staff gained greater skill in working with problems of intrapsychic conflict.

In the course of its history ALCS was frequently asked whether it was indeed a social agency offering casework counseling or was it merely using the cloak of a social agency format to enable practitioners to practice psychotherapy in competition with psychology and psychiatry. The best answer is to be found in a review of ALCS statistics.

Figures for the decade ending in 1969 reveal that 41 to 53 percent (but generally less than 50 percent) of the clients who telephoned terminated contact after that inquiry. This drop-out rate is high but it is comparable to the rate in most social agencies. [79]  About 13 percent of the clients who called had one interview; 14 percent had from two to five interviews; and 28 percent terminated contact only after six or more interviews. [80]  Of those who had at least six interviews, 15 to 20 percent in any year terminated after 95 or more interviews. The proportion of ALCS clients who had at least six interviews was higher than that of at least one philanthropic, voluntary agency whose experience was shared with us. Nevertheless, 27 percent *were* served in five or fewer interviews.

It cannot be assumed that these clients were unmotivated to use long-term help or that the practitioners were "thwarted" in doing "long-term psychotherapy." A sample study of outcome of treatment, based on practitioner judgments for a two-year period (July 1, 1965 through June 30, 1967), indicates that 38 percent of those who terminated after two to five interviews were judged to have benefited in their understanding of their situation and ability to cope with it, or that the specific need which brought them to the agency had been met. [81]

Thus in answer to the question of similarity or dissimilarity of types of requests clients brought to ALCS as compared with those brought by clients of other social agencies, one can say that there was no difference. The counseling services they required and received were the same as those in other social agencies, with the possible exception of ALCS staff engagement in prolonged psychotherapeutic intervention. In providing the latter, ALCS accepted the professional responsibility of extending staff competence through a self-imposed advanced training program. *The result was the development of greater compe-*

*tence at all levels of practice.*

A number of ALCS clients requested aid (at intake or in the course of contact) in securing a variety of "concrete" services, such as special educational programs for the handicapped or for disturbed children, housing for the aged or mentally ill, temporary care of children, and so forth. Clients were asked what they had done in the past to meet such situations and what services they had used. How adequate were the resources they had used? Would they need or respond to the resources offered or used by social agencies?

The target clientele did indeed need such help. In the past they had often used boarding schools rather than foster homes for children, residential hotels for elderly members of a family or for persons discharged from mental hospitals, and companions and homemakers to provide either temporary or permanent care for elderly persons who wanted to remain in their own homes, and occasionally for children. They had sought this help through a variety of employment agencies or through individual advertising. By and large, they had not turned to social agencies for services of this nature.

Earlier we mentioned ALCS use of Adult Counselors and Home Finders to give these kinds of service to ALCS clients. [82] On·the basis of their experience and ALCS collaboration with them, it was clearly established that the middle- and upper-income client needs the help of a professional who is skilled in evaluating resources. Any family can advertise, for example, for a companion for an elderly person or can learn of existing schools or institutions. They cannot so readily assess the applicant for a position or the institution in relation to the specific needs of a family member. Often they are too involved to remain objective and they are inclined to make compromises that do not work out. In addition, social work can offer its skills in

helping the individual, his family, and the resource during
the initial period of adjustment. Many social workers have
assumed that the financially advantaged client who can
pay for service does not need such help in locating or evaluating resources for the special needs of family members.
ALCS experience would indicate that he does need such
help and will use the skills of the social work profession
if they are made available to him.

In its 1963 report to the Board of Directors, the Technical Advisory Committee suggested that ALCS caution
agencies interested in extending their services to the
economically advantaged that New York City is an atypical
community owing to its wealth of resources. [83]   Other
communities interested in establishing services for upper-
income clients will need to review their own resources in
relation to the availability of experienced casework practitioners, of staff training facilities, and of a host of
ancillary services.

### Was Support Through Fees Achieved?

The final question set for the pilot program was whether
service of a high caliber could be supported solely through
client fees. Within three years, it was apparent that the
answer to this question was yes. Although the agency's
client service program was primarily supported by the
Adele and Arthur Lehman Foundation grant during these
years, fees accounted for an increasing percentage of income. The grant supplemented the income from fees until
1960-61, but thereafter fees covered the full cost.

The achievement of self-support must be viewed, however, in relation to such factors as the adequacy of staff
compensation and the cost of consultation and in-service
training. [84]   It was reported earlier that the practitioners' base salary rose in *actual* dollars from $6,000 in
1954 to $20,000 in July, 1969. Annual practitioner income

was more than that because of payment for extra interviews and (for a few years) the year-end adjustment. A rough estimate for the ten-year period 1958-59 through 1968-69 indicates that practitioner income increased by 62 percent in *constant* dollars. During approximately the same period, the median income of New York City's white families rose by 20 percent [85] and the salaries of senior caseworkers in the voluntary agencies of New York City rose, in *constant* dollars, by 42 percent. Fees rose during the 15½ years by 41 percent, which was slightly higher than the 37 percent rise in the Consumer Price Index for all goods and services in the New York City region. [86]

The amount spent for consultations and seminars rose from $2,800 in 1954 to $10,100 in 1968-69. To some extent the expense for consultation was influenced by the number of practitioners, but it increased also as staff became clearer about the additional training they needed. (The peak size of ALCS staff occurred in 1963-64.) It would appear, then, that self-support was not achieved at the expense of the staff's need for an adequate salary or their wish to improve the quality of their service.

What accounts for ALCS success in the area of full agency support from fees? One factor was the ability, with experience, to identify and assess unit costs—a relatively simple matter since it involved only the service of counseling, defined in its broad context which ranges from giving of information to psychotherapy. Another factor was the relatively large volume of service an experienced staff could handle without detriment to quality. Though staff productivity was high, it may not have been higher than that of equally experienced staff in other agencies. (The Technical Advisory Committee believed the "incentive" pay plan was a factor in high productivity.) To these factors must be added the staff's feeling of professional responsibility for achieving the goal of self-support. In spite of the strains that developed over the salary issue, at no point did the board and staff differ concerning the validity of this goal for the agency.

Another factor was the affluence of the client group, though affluence is no guarantee that a client will pay the fee. Therefore, client satisfaction with the kind and quality of service rendered must also have been an important factor in producing income and achieving self-support. The staff had a deep conviction that the client's pattern of fee payment revealed his conscious or unconscious expectations of others, his sense of himself, as well as his reactions to treatment in general, or the specific treatment he was receiving. Undoubtedly, the staff's prompt handling of a client's failure to pay the fee, within the context of its potential treatment implications, was an important factor in the high rate of fee collection.

In summary, the ALCS experience indicates that with an initial subsidy to initiate the program, casework service of a high caliber can be provided to middle- and upper-income clients at full-cost fees, without creating a financial burden for the community. [87]

### Did ALCS Program Provide Incentive for Other Agencies?

It will be recalled that the hope of the founding group and the board was that the program would serve as an incentive for the establishment of similar services in many communities. Without such a growth, the objective of changing the public's view of social work from that of a philanthropic endeavor to that of a professional service could not be realized. It was not until 1957, when it was clear that the target clientele needed and would use casework services, that ALCS began to assess its role in encouraging the extension of similar programs outside New York City.

A number of the board members favored the agency's taking an active role. The Technical Advisory Committee suggested that ALCS set up a full-cost service in another city to strengthen the validity of its findings. It was also proposed that ALCS convene agencies in various cities, both to inform them of ALCS experience and to encourage their attempting to set up similar programs. It was further suggested that ALCS conduct a three-day workshop in New York City for lay leaders and executives of family agencies, inviting some of them to serve on the ALCS Board of Directors. However, most of the board members favored a less active role, believing that it was the task of the profession to promote similar programs; if professional social workers enthusiastically supported the expansion of these services, initial funding would be found and lay support would be forthcoming. Therefore, without any formal vote, the decision was made to be available for consultation, to answer inquiries, to continue to operate the ALCS's own program, and to inform the social work profession through whatever means was available.

Only three agencies, *whose intent was to extend services to the middle- and upper-income groups in their communities,* consulted ALCS, each over a period of years. [88] It must be understood that these agencies, like most, served anyone who applied, but they agreed that, in all probability, the target clientele did not use their services in larger numbers because of the conditions under which services were offered. They also believed that increasing the number of middle- and upper-income clients might lead to greater public understanding of their services (free and subsidized) and thus to increased financial support for their agencies.

Two of these agencies did open a full-cost service unit, attached to their existing agency program but distinguished by a special name. [89] All three consulted ALCS while making a decision about the potential value to them of extending service to the groups ALCS had reached. They raised a number of questions: What caliber of staff would be required? Would they need to be as experienced as ALCS's? What public relations program was recommended? How were fees to be set to assure full support? What funds were necessary to initiate such a program?

Only one agency asked for help in integrating its new program into the existing one, particularly in relation to revising policies, deploying staff and handling staff reactions. This agency had established the unit with an inadequate budget and therefore with a serious handicap in reaching and serving the target clientele. The agency was located in a deteriorating neighborhood, although there were plans for its relocation, which could not be carried out for several years. Though the board and executive doubted that the target client group would come to the agency, they were unable to secure enough money to rent space in a more desirable neighborhood. The program "petered out," and when a new executive director was employed, the agency returned to its former method of serving middle- and upper-income clients. Currently some clients pay a full-cost fee since the agency fee scale has no set limit. Another reason given for disbanding the unit was that the agency had become increasingly involved with what it saw as its service priority: finding ways of reaching and serving severely impoverished minority groups.

The second agency began with an excellent subsidy from an individual and the enthusiastic support of the executive director and a nucleus of board members. They were convinced that the affluent, suburban population needed a family counseling program and that eventually such a program would increase community understanding, use, and support of all the agency's philanthropic services. This program has been successful. Within a year, its "full-cost" service was supported totally by income from fees.

The third consulted ALCS first by mail and eventually through personal contact and a two-day consultation visit. This agency is located in an affluent community, in which there is only a small percentage of low-income residents. Therefore, they saw logic in doing something to attract and serve the majority of their population, but so far they have not moved in this direction. At the time of the consultation, several concerns were expressed. How could they secure adequate initial funding? Would the Community Chest gradually withdraw funds they needed to serve those who required free or subsidized service? The representative of the Community Chest, who participated in the consultation feared that the establishment and publicizing of services to middle- and upper-income clients would detrimentally affect the annual fund-raising drive and result in curtailment of all social services for the lower-income groups. [90]  To what extent these concerns account for the agency's making no changes is not known; but it appeared that the board and executive were not really ready to take the step of changing from the agency's traditional philanthropic role. Perhaps this was related to the fact that there was insufficient support for the idea among the agency's professional staff and other professional workers in the community. They viewed the concerns expressed as insurmountable obstacles rather than as factors to be faced and dealt with in setting up services for a new client group.

ALCS also received many requests for specific information, not directly related to opening a similar resource for clients. These came from family and child guidance agencies, lay leaders in social work, individuals in private practice wishing to open group private practices, and hospital social service departments or medical group practices and medical centers. Most of the questions had to do with fees— how they were set, what ALCS fees were, and whether they did meet full costs of operating the agency. Family agencies seemed most concerned about fees as a potential source of income to continue their current program rather than as a means of extending services to this particular unserved client group. Nor were they interested in changing the public image of social work. This was not as true of inquiries received from hospital social service departments or medical centers. Here the interest seemed to be more in how one could reach or attract these potential clients. Perhaps this is because the medical social worker comes in direct contact with an economic cross-section of the community and has the direct experiences of seeing that illness creates problems for patients and their families regardless of economic status.

The ALCS hope of enlisting the interest of other social agencies in reinterpreting social work as a profession has not been fulfilled. This may be because social workers lack conviction that the public's view of social work materially affects the support and use of social services. Or it may be that a response was expected too soon. Judging from ALCS experience in talking with boards of other social agencies, it appears that many have yet to comprehend the possibility that a social agency need not be totally philanthropic. The concept of social services as social utilities has not been advanced among some of them.

Another reason for failure in this regard may be related to timing. The ALCS program began in 1954, shortly before the profession again became primarily concerned with its role in the alleviation or elimination of social ills. Its traditional concern with and responsibility for severely disadvantaged groups, helping them deal with powerful social and economic forces, was intensified by the proliferation of social ills, their increased intensity, and their encroachment on the lives of everyone, regardless of economic status. The profession returned to consideration of the need for broad social planning and of the part social work could play, along with other professional disciplines, in such planning. This trend was accompanied, however, by discrediting of individualized services, as if one had to choose between social action and individual casework.

There seems, however, at this point to be some recognition of the need for broad, preventive planning, better utilization of existing resources and expanded provision of services to families and individuals. A more balanced view of what social action and casework can each contribute may evolve. If it does, social agencies will return to the question of services for individuals and families, to whether they will serve only the economically disadvantaged or have some responsibility to make their services available to persons from all economic strata. In either event, they will need to give thought to how *all* the unserved groups in any community can be reached and how services will be financed. At that point, the experience of ALCS may be useful in answering questions concerning services for middle- and upper-income clients.

The professional social work scene has changed since 1954, particularly in the change in the professional status of the private practitioner. In 1954 there were few private practitioners, many of whom did not identify themselves as social workers. By and large, they were ignored by the profession, which neither recognized them as social workers nor repudiated them. But today the profession has increasingly come to recognize that the private practice of social work is legitimate and that the private practitioner is also deeply concerned about high standards for practice and the need for broad-scale preventive planning. As the official arm of the profession, the National Association of Social Workers now includes private practitioners in the pursuit of common professional goals. It has taken steps to identify the qualifications needed by practitioners in order to practice independently, whether in an agency or in private practice. It has moved toward assuming a protective role toward social work's clients through its current program of certification of competence, its increased efforts to achieve licensing for social workers, and its concern with the establishment of a means of regulating practice, whether in an agency or by a private practitioner. These efforts may lessen the concern of social workers about referring clients to private practitioners, who in the future may become the main source of social work services to the middle- and upper-income client groups. It may even be that ALCS's aim of furthering the public's understanding of social work as a profession will be fulfilled by private practitioners rather than by social agencies.

ALCS observed that some people will not go to a private practitioner because they have greater trust in the quality of service given by an agency or a group practice. Some of them believe that an agency offers them the added value of peer consultation, of having more than one expert's knowledge used in their behalf. Some cite the importance of a group of lay leaders who, as objective observers, can attest to the agency's high practice standards. On the other hand, some people never use the services of a social agency or group practice, again for a variety of reasons, such as concern over confidentiality, fantasies that there will be a more personal approach and concern for them as individuals from a private practitioner, and confusion between quality and fees charged. But regardless of the validity of the reasons offered by those who prefer either a private practitioner or an agency, what is important is that these serve as obstacles to seeking and using needed help. It is obvious, therefore, that every community needs a variety of resources for social casework services to facilitate the early reaching out for help. To provide such a variety of resources is in keeping with social work's responsibility to enable potential clients to find and use services.

One hypothesis of the founding group was that the programs of social agencies would improve if agencies did scrve all economic groups. We expected that ALCS clients, as members of an economic group that gives financial support to social agencies, would demand that such agencies give a high quality of service. This demand would result from their having themselves been in the client role. Having experienced good service, they would be less inclined to support financially an agency whose services were poor. Thus the effect of serving the middle- and upper-income client would be the elevation of the quality of the social agency's services for *all* clients. ALCS experience with this hypothesis, which needs further validation, points in the direction of its being correct.

# 4. *Structure and the Issue of Accountability*

SO FAR, in presenting the findings of this pilot venture, we have discussed the aims of the pilot project in relation to the clientele reached, the goal of agency self-support, and the hope of the founding group to further the public's understanding of casework as a professional discipline through influencing other agencies to respond to the needs of a wider clientele than they were then serving. But as the title of this report indicates, the ALCS experience offers a "case history of structure and accountability." What follows is a detailed analysis of changes in agency structure and accountability as they evolved during the life of ALCS. It includes what was learned from ALCS's changes in the traditional roles of board and staff because of its pertinence to the current redefining of board and professional staff roles and responsibilities as related to the milieu in which social agencies now operate. The ALCS experience may have most direct implications for the voluntary family agency.

It has been stated previously that the structure of an agency reflects its concept of accountability: to whom, for what, and through which component units. Because of the original hypothesis about the mature, experienced practitioner, ALCS started with a departure from traditional structure by eliminating supervision. [91]  Later it was found necessary to make other changes as the client pay-

ment of full-cost fees began to have an impact on the roles
and responsibilities of the agency's component units. ALCS
offers an example of one theory of supervision and its goal
of professional maturity. It also provides a case example of
the relationship between the source of income and the
structure required for the fulfillment of accountability,
which, it is hoped, can be useful in the development of
hypotheses to be tested by other agencies as they face
similar changes.

In reporting how the changes in structure and in consequent roles affected the ALCS board, executive and staff,
it is important to observe that all were representative of
board members and professional social workers reared in
the era of the 1930s to the 1950s. All were socialized to
the fulfillment of designated tasks at a time when voluntary agencies were still supported chiefly by large, individual donors (although United Funds and Federations had
begun to tap contributions from broader groups). The professional services were rendered through agency structures
built upon the same concept as were the early social agencies; philanthropy was the motivating factor. Governmental
programs were a new phenomenon although they grew rapidly during this time. The concept of the *rights* of individuals adversely affected by social and economic changes
had gained no more than a toehold. These aspects of the
era are important to note because it is likely that similar
transitional discomforts may be experienced by some boards
and staffs today—even those socialized in the 1960s. They,
too, will find that the structure of the social agency has to
be modified if it is to be relevant to the concepts and trends
of today's society.

### Supervision, Quality of Service and Accountability

The decision to eliminate supervision was implicit in the
thinking about how the agency might best be set up to

attract the target clientele and to conduct a sound pilot program. It was believed that hiring a highly experienced staff and promoting a team relationship called for the elimination of supervision. This decision also provided the opportunity to test out a hypothesis concerning the optimum conditions under which a practitioner can perform at the highest level of his competence. As a part of this hypothesis, the ultimate goal of supervision was viewed as the preparation of the practitioner for his eventual assumption of accountability for the quality of his service to clients. (The term "preparation" is used to encompass a process of learning with decreasing dependence upon supervision, which enables the practitioner eventually to internalize aspects of accountability as his self-expectations. Such internalization is one of the hallmarks of full professional competence.) Since ALCS had hired a highly experienced staff, it was felt that each member had a direct, professional accountability for the quality of his service to his clients, and that supervision therefore was unnecessary.

This decision evoked considerable interest on the part of social workers in ALCS. It seems to have created much greater interest than did the hope of changing the public's view of social work. Although the latter was seen as desirable, it had less connection with the immediate experience of most social workers. In the 1950s supervision was a major issue of professional debate:

*Could supervision ever terminate or was it an essential part of agency accountability to its "community"?*

*Did supervision foster dependence and hinder professional maturation?*

*Was independence the desired goal of professional training or was it, perhaps, interdependence since social work was to be practiced in institutional settings?*

*Was the practitioner a professional person accountable to the agency for the fulfillment of defined responsibilities, but to himself and his clients for the quality of practice he gave?*

*Could the two responsibilities of supervision—educating the practitioner for a professional role and ensuring adequate service to client and community—be separated, or were they so interwoven that one could not be achieved without the other?*

*Could one really count on even the most competent practitioner to continue to strive to keep his skills and knowledge at a high level, or to be interested in advanced learning and training, if the support and stimulation of supervision were removed?*

These were questions that were discussed at length in professional articles, at national conferences, and in a variety of seminars. The same questions were posed to ALCS by colleagues outside of the agency.

At present supervision does not appear to command the same interest of the profession, at least not in open debate. However, it remains an integral part of educating for the practice of social work. It also remains an integral part of the administrative process of providing client service. Agencies, therefore, must still raise the same questions. A recent development, however, is extremely important—the Academy of Certified Social Workers (ACSW) program of certification for competence under the aegis of NASW. It will undoubtedly bring forth again questions of accountability for quality of service and the role of supervision. Who is accountable? Who determines who can carry the accountability inherent in "independent" practice—agency or professional organization? The ALCS experience thus may offer a useful case example as the debate continues.

The response of the profession to elimination of supervision for a mature staff was both positive and negative. Those who favored the ALCS decision believed that the goal of supervision was the practitioner's eventual assumption of full accountability for his work and that, indeed, this independence was the hallmark of professional maturity. ALCS was commended for having taken a long overdue step. On the other hand, many felt that the transfer to the practitioner of full accountability for the quality of his practice was not possible and that the Board of Directors and the Executive Director were evading their responsibilities. To restate the ALCS position briefly: the executive's and board's accountability for quality of service rested in the *selection of staff who met the criteria of professional maturity*, with its implications of current competence and continued interest in maintaining skills at the highest level possible. [92]  In addition, responsibility was assumed for creating a milieu or a structure consistent with what was expected of the staff. The structure had to be one that would permit and support the independence of the practitioner. Thus responsibility had not been evaded, rather the respective accountability of administration and practitioner had been redefined. What was the experience with this decision? How did board, executive and staff react to their new roles and their accountability for quality of service? What readjustments were necessary for each to make? Does the ALCS experience point to the validity of the hypothesis? We shall attempt to answer these questions, dealing first with the apparent reactions of the board.

## 1.  Board Reactions

The board did not appear to have any discomfort in shifting to the staff full accountability for the quality of service. Board members were interested in the methods of staff selection, in how staff reacted to being independent, and the readjustments staff had to make. When the agenda of a board meeting included presentation of professional issues concerned with quality of service, members asked astute questions and challenged inadequate answers as only an experienced and well-informed group can. Their purpose, however, was to keep informed and to act as catalysts for the achievement of clarity (if only for the purpose of interpretation) rather than to direct, decide or control professional decisions.

The reasons for the board's ease in having accountability for quality of service vested in the practitioner are probably many and some can only be conjectured. However, it must be remembered that the board comprised a group of laymen who had had many years of experience with excellent social agencies. They had learned how difficult it is to make professional decisions and were aware of the intricacy of the matters to be weighed. Therefore, they did not believe that even informed laymen were capable of making them. Most of them believed that the quality of service given a client could not be regulated by structure itself. In the last analysis, they saw service quality as dependent upon the integrity of the practitioner, his pride in his work, and his inner need to serve others well. Certainly all of them were reassured by the staff qualifications that had been set, by the selection process and by the caliber of those selected. It can be conjectured, however, that some members of the board experienced no change in their feeling of accountability for quality of service. Their confidence in the quality of service offered was derived primarily from their appraisal of the professional commitment and judgment of the Executive Director. One member of the ALCS board said she was confident about the agency's professional service because "I know you wouldn't tolerate shoddy practice."

## 2.  Staff Reactions

The staff had two kinds of reactions to their newly defined roles. The first can be called "transitional" problems. All staff, regular or evening, and regardless of the time of their appointment, reported that in the beginning they experienced a heightened concern about their practice. It was as if the loss of usual agency supports (defined policies and guidelines, supervision, and so forth) was experienced as a loss in their assurance of their own competence. What they described is not unlike what has been described in the social work literature of an earlier period about caseworkers' reactions to the initiation of fee-charging. [93] The introduction of fees made caseworkers begin to question what they had to offer and whether they were fully prepared. At ALCS the question was whether they were fully prepared to practice independently. This initial reaction was soon followed, however, by a sense of pleasure both with the responsibility they carried and the freedom it gave them to make decisions, to test out hypotheses, and use or discard ideas as they tried to be as helpful as possible to their clients. The experience of responsible freedom served to increase their self-respect and confidence.

Another transitional problem was confined primarily to those staff members appointed within the first two years. They reported discomfort in their relationship to each other in an agency without supervision. They became aware that in other social agencies they had viewed responsibility for the quality of a colleague's practice as belonging to someone in the administrative structure. When they had given consultation to their colleagues in other agencies, they had expected the colleague's supervisor to be the one to deal with his more personal problems if they were interfering with his practice. When they continued to give evidence of a similar expectation of the Executive Director, she called it to their attention. [94] Out of the discussions of the inappropriateness of this expectation, the group became aware that they felt that their own reputations were dependent upon the practice and reputations of all members of the group. This concern led to a closer examination of what was different in a group practice. The conclusion reached was that when a consultation was requested, those consulted put at the disposal of the person asking for help their collective knowledge and competence on behalf of the client. *Consultation in a group practice had the characteristic of total momentary investment in offering the client* (along with the colleague requesting help) *the benefit of the collective knowledge, observation and skills of the group.* Once the consultation was over, however, it remained the responsibility of the practitioner to determine how he would use what was offered him, in the light of his own experience with the client. No subsequent accounting to the group was required but he could request additional consultation. The outcome of these discussions was a greater sense of a group practice. Staff also had a clearer concept of the need for their involvement in reviewing and defining the criteria for staff selection and in the process of selection itself.

Perhaps staff appointed in later years did not have this problem because the first group had worked it through and the milieu was different. Later practitioners learned that no one withheld whatever he could offer and no one expected him to do more than weigh their ideas against his own clinical experience. No one attempted to supervise him. The group's investment was serving the client well.

Once the practitioner internalized the meaning of "independent practice," he was able to cope with his new role and responsibilities. We shall see in some detail how this came about, because professional colleagues raised many questions about shifting accountability for practice to the practitioner himself. One question asked was whether staff did indeed show evidence of a desire to raise the level of their knowledge and skills in the absence of supervision. It must be remembered that no provision had been made for periodic administrative review of a practitioner's work. With few exceptions, treatment decisions were left entirely to the practitioner. Moreover, no provision had been made for an in-service training program, although ALCS did provide three consultants. It also set aside funds to cover the cost of whatever the staff felt was necessary to ensure practice of high quality. From 1958 on there was not even a limit on the number of extra interviews each practitioner would be allowed to carry. Therefore, the question of how a skilled and experienced staff reacts to such freedom is an important one.

What constitutes evidence that a practitioner has a continuing interest in raising the level of his practice? Customarily, evidence that he is engaging in ongoing professional self-evaluation or self-assessment is to be found in his seeking consultation, making innovations in treatment, reading the professional literature, taking advanced training courses, writing professional articles, and/or engaging in research. Let us look at each of these processes as they were reflected in the performance of ALCS practitioners.

It will be recalled that part of the two staff meetings a week was given over to consultation. The administrative meeting was used for *peer consultation.* In the psychiatric meeting there were peer consultation and psychiatric consultation combined. The consultants in internal medicine and psychology were called on by staff as individual client situations dictated the need, and only a few meetings were held with each of these consultants over the years. Such meetings were held when the consultants could report new developments related to ALCS practice. Sparse use was made of the consultant in medicine. Those who had had experience in medical settings often suggested to their colleagues that a medical consultation might be helpful, and when a consultation was held, the staff found it rewarding. Therefore, the only conjecture that can be made as to the sparseness of the use of the medical consultant is that experience in social agencies does not help the practitioner understand the contribution of such a consultant to the same extent that it helps him understand the contribution of the consultant in psychology or psychiatry. The consultant in psychology was used primarily for discussion of the meaning of the results of psychological testing. Staff were interested in increasing their understanding of the significance of test results, copies of which the consultant provided along with her conclusions.

Peer consultations began in a somewhat traditional fashion with staff asking for help in dealing with difficult client situations. Eventually the group agreed that it was also important to present unusual or interesting client situations so that a worker's experience—for example, with an ethnic group and the effect of ethnicity on treatment—could be shared with everyone. Later, however, consultations concerning individual client situations were excluded from the administrative meeting. Instead, such were sought from one colleague or a small group of colleagues. It became customary for a specific time to be set aside by the person (or persons) approached for a consultation to assure that enough time could be given to understand the problem fully and offer appropriate help.

Peer consultations continued throughout the history of the agency. At the end of two different years, staff members were asked whether they had held any peer consultations. All had done so, and it was obvious that the consultations had been sought because the colleague selected was viewed as having particular qualities or assets. One practitioner was considered to be unusually creative; another had special knowledge derived from a previous job experience; another was viewed as being unusually perceptive; and yet another seemed to have extensive knowledge of psychoanalytic theory. Some were seen as being very helpful during a period of waiting out the results of a difficult treatment choice because they had empathy but did not give advice or false assurance. Therefore, which colleague one chose as a consultant depended not only on the need for a consultation but also on the person's special contribution or special quality.

Consultation with the psychiatrist began in 1954 with the whole group participating. Each meeting also included exploration of a professional question, usually one that arose out of the consultation or had been stirred up by someone's attendance at a professional meeting or reading of a professional article. While these meetings were interesting and rewarding in many ways because they were educational, the group began to be dissatisfied with them, perhaps because they lacked focus.

In the early years (1954-57) one or another of the group raised questions from time to time about the referral of a particular client to a psychiatrist for treatment. In some instances the referral had been made and the client had either not followed through or had stopped psychiatric treatment and had returned to the practitioner. Often the reason given for having made the referral was that the client's treatment needs were "outside the scope of social work competence." The consultant's questions about the meaning of this phrase forced a closer examination of it and resulted in many heated discussions about the limitations of social work. Each became aware of a number of assumptions in social work that he had never challenged: for example, the assumption that there was a clear-cut definition of the respective roles of psychology, psychiatry and social work in psychotherapy and that this definition was concurred in by all three professions. This assumption was not valid [95] and at best one could only say that a truce existed. It was assumed that social work's role in psychotherapy could not change—in contrast to the concept of its role in social planning. None had examined whether the goal of improved social functioning, which is said to be the goal of social work, can really be achieved solely through the interventive methods traditionally taught in schools of social work and followed in many agencies. Was improvement in social functioning possible, for example, if intrapsychic conflicts prevented change? The conclusion was reached that the discomfort in serving clients was due to weaknesses in curricula of schools of social work and in experience as workers in agencies—lacks which inhibited the staff in the practice of psychotherapy. Schools of social work teach persons the basic skills needed to enter practice. In-service education programs increase these skills. However, these were and are limited by the accepted definition of what is "within the scope of social work competence and methods" and the lack of challenge of this definition. Therefore, instead of accepting the prohibition to seek additional knowledge, the staff engaged in a process of advanced training to extend the sphere of competence in helping clients move toward the goal of improved social functioning.

The first lack in staff knowledge for which *additional education was undertaken* was how better to help the client who needed "long-term psychotherapy." This was defined as the client whose ability to cope with daily life responsibilities and tasks required the resolution of those intrapsychic problems that inhibited growth and kept him from changing his patterns of response to individuals or situations. This was not as clearly conceptualized at first and staff were unsure about the preparation they needed. But eventually they defined the need as a more extensive and minute understanding of ego development and personality growth as well as how to use various interventive methods in a more sophisticated manner. The consultant in psychiatry advised an education program with someone skilled in psychotherapy and he secured such a consultant for this purpose.

A few members of the staff involved in "long-term treatment" with one or two clients engaged in the new program on an experimental basis. They agreed to report to the whole group after they had had some experience with it.

Difficult to define, the educational process which evolved joined elements of both consultation and tutorial education. The consultant reviewed with the practitioner over a period of time the latter's weekly contacts with one or more clients involved in long-term treatment. He would also recommend reading that would increase the practitioner's knowledge in a specific area. His consultation drew on his own method and experience, but his objective was teaching the practitioner rather than controlling, directing or sharing in the responsibility for the treatment of the client. The practitioner still remained responsible for using whatever the consultant offered. Staff reported that this experience deepened their understanding of the process of treatment, helped them identify the various levels that they had to be aware of, and gave them a greater sense of understanding of what the client was experiencing and communicating than they had had previously. Subsequently it was decided that all staff members would have a similar period of education. It seemed possible at the time that staff might actually be seeking another form of supervision, but this concern was not borne out by experience. The practitioner did remain responsible for his treatment decisions. The length of this training varied from individual to individual, but never exceeded one year.

A number of staff members had enrolled in courses and seminars offered through various institutes for psychotherapy in New York City. (One took such courses with the aim of qualifying for lay psychotherapy, but the rest did not have this goal.) Obviously, accountability for quality of work did not require the stimulation of being supervised but only motivation to serve clients well. At first, staff members enrolled in courses on their own and paid for them. Apparently they viewed gaps in their knowledge as unique to themselves and their own responsibility to remedy. It was inevitable, however, that in staff meetings or informal contacts they would share information gained in a seminar or course. They also reported that the content of most courses offered through the institutes for psychotherapy was geared primarily to individual therapy and to clients who had some recognition that the problem was their own, in contrast to the clients who seek social agency help. The staff's dissatisfaction with these courses and the fact that they were seeking similar knowledge content led to the use of the psychiatric meeting time for a seminar program. A number of brief seminars were held and various psychiatrists were engaged as leaders. Such leaders did bring depth of knowledge in a particular area, but some of them also held preconceived and delimiting ideas of what social workers do and therefore what they need to learn.

In 1962, an analyst was selected by staff and conducted seminars through 1969. Staff always determined the focus of the seminars. [96]   Largely because of the format, the seminars produced unexpected benefits. One week the group would discuss assigned reading material related to their interests for the purpose of clarifying theory as well as understanding the specific contribution of the reading material to the therapeutic problem under examination. The second week a practitioner would present a case from his own practice to illuminate the theory discussed the week before. This format provided a valuable interweaving of theory and suggested interventive methods within the realities of actual practice. In addition, it made staff take a different interest in reading. Material was no longer skimmed but read and re-read to increase understanding of its contribution to practice. Staff requested additions to the agency library because so many of them, simultaneously, were reading and re-reading the same material. Another benefit of this format was the opportunity it provided for valuable peer exchange, which always dealt with significant professional issues about which there were disagreements. These differences, viewed in the wider perspective of a theoretical discussion (rather than the handling of a specific client) did in effect help each learn from the others in the group. Perhaps this was because there was none of the tensions that often accompany the direct review of one's practice even in consultations.

Despite this common training, each practitioner continued to seek additional opportunities for learning. Some wanted a series of consultations with a psychiatrist or an expert in a related field; some continued to enroll in courses or seminars offered in centers for psychotherapy. One staff member expressed the feeling that there was a distinct difference in how he sought additional preparation while at ALCS in contrast with his other work settings. Previously he had enrolled in courses to gain knowledge, unavailable through his agency's in-service education program, motivated by some new development in the field, not necessarily related to his practice at the time. At ALCS, the necessity of carrying full accountability for his practice had made him more conscious of the need for selecting courses which would contribute to building a firm conceptual base for his practice. He believed that this was equally true for all staff members and accounted for their ability to tolerate and benefit from each other's views even in the heat of debate over differences.

Staff were also alert to all new developments in the field. For example, they arranged a seminar with a leading expert in family interviewing. [97] Similarly, a number of authorities on group counseling were consulted. [98] Consultations, however, were conducted somewhat like seminars, involving advanced reading as well as exchange on the methods and aims of group counseling. Subsequently one consultant was asked to help ALCS formulate a group counseling program for marital pairs. The person selected was considered to have the knowledge and experience most directly related to the use of group counseling in a social agency. [99]

Concern over the difficult treatment problems presented by some clients inevitably led individual practitioners to undertake *experimentation or innovation.* These variations in practice were always initiated by the practitioner since no prior approval was needed even if additional costs were involved as, for example, in taping and transcription of interviews, or in the use of special consultants. Each professional eventually reached a point where he needed to test out his initial hypotheses as well as his beginning deductions from his experimentation and the entire group would become involved. These experimentations or innovations had elements of research in that the practitioner had a hypothesis from which a plan of intervention flowed, he planned the means of review and evaluation, and he presented his work to his colleagues for their reactions.

Generally speaking, ALCS staff did not voluntarily write papers for publication, although they did some writing when papers were asked for by state or national conferences or some other professional group. [100]

Staff shared the Executive Director's conviction that an agency of mature practitioners had a special obligation to engage in research and contribute to the body of professional knowledge. The very length of their experience and the depth of their knowledge were potential assets in undertaking relatively sophisticated research. Yet it was not possible to secure their collaboration in initiating a research program.

In 1962, Dr. David Fanshel expressed interest in doing research in relation to casework treatment. [101] Because this was close to staff interests, the Executive Director discussed his appointment with the Administrative Committee of the board, at the same time commenting that the staff did not appear ready to be involved. Since, however, such an appointment might be necessary before a research program could be instituted, the Administrative Committee agreed to it and funds were secured from the Adele and Arthur Lehman Foundation for a three-year period.

The Executive Director informed the staff of Dr. Fanshel's appointment and the area of his interest but did not ask them to concur with the decision to appoint him. They understood that his research proposal would be discussed with them and that each could decide whether he wished to participate. Dr. Fanshel did secure staff cooperation in the development of his proposal. First, however, he and the staff had to become accustomed to each other's terminology. Differences in the meaning of technical terms created tensions and doubts both about whether to engage in research and whether research would actually be possible. It took time for Dr. Fanshel and the staff to trust each other's commitment both to sound practice and to the contribution of research to professional knowledge. When a proposal was submitted and funds were secured, four members of the staff had already agreed to participate. The others did not, primarily because the study required the client's consent to having interviews taped consistently over a period of months and they believed that this would affect treatment adversely. [102]

Research in a formal sense was not initiated in collaboration with staff. Whether eventually staff would have collaborated in initiating research cannot now be answered. It would appear that practitioners find it hard to accept the intervention of certain kinds of research in the treatment process, particularly when the project requires consistent and conscious participation by the client. Research does not always appear to the client to have any direct relevance to the problem for which he sought help. This can cause him to question the essential motive in serving him. It can make him reluctant to share pertinent information or discuss important experiences because of his fantasies about the reactions of unknown researchers. The continuing research review of interviews with clients still in treatment can also make the practitioner somewhat self-conscious in the subsequent interview with a client, creating a stilted atmosphere and thereby hampering treatment. Nevertheless, in retrospect it would seem none of the professional staff had been sufficiently prepared in this aspect of accountability to the profession to be able to assume this role easily. With today's greater acceptance of research as an integral part of agency practice, perhaps the social worker of the future will have more understanding of the rigors of research and therefore be more at ease with it. If the knowledge base of the profession is to be built, validated research is essential, and agencies are potentially among the richest resources for pragmatic observation and evaluation.

One final point to be commented on in regard to quality of practice attained by the ALCS staff is the relationship between quality of practice and the maintenance of a high rate of interview production. It should be recalled that no limitation was set on the number of extra interviews a practitioner was allowed to have. It was understood that the individual's production would remain consistent with sound practice and with the fulfillment of other responsibilities, such as attendance at and full participation in staff meetings, particularly those related to the administration of the agency. Recording, collateral visits, and so forth, were included in the ALCS definition of sound practice.
[103]

Earlier it was stated that the minimum expectation of production set by the staff was 1,210 interviews per year. In actuality, by 1969 all practitioners were holding 200 "extra" interviews per year. While the steady increase in productivity may have been partially due to the "incentive pay," as suggested by the Technical Advisory Committee, it was also related to the added years of experience and the steady advance in knowledge gained from added training, which resulted in a growing sense of practitioner confidence in his ability to help clients. Individual variations in productivity reflected individual patterns in the use of work and leisure time and in the level of physical energy and the variations in personal responsibilities for children and family. Variations also occurred from year to year for each staff member. A worker might have a higher interview count one year because he had decided to confine his additional training to the agency seminars. By the same token, he might have fewer interviews another year because he was also taking courses outside the agency and needed more time for the reading required. A practitioner might plan a longer vacation one year, or reduce it the next year to earn more money. Sometimes a practitioner curtailed his production to devote more time to unrelated study because he wished to expand his horizons in other than social work areas, or because he wanted to engage in an extracurricular activity such as consultation to a nursery school.

There was no evidence that a high interview count was maintained at the cost of quality of practice. One must recall that increased production coincided with an increased commitment to advanced training. The general impression is that no practitioner had an excessive interest in money per se. Each had his own concept of a sound balance between work and leisure and he valued this balance more than increased income.

In summary, it is evident that the ALCS staff assumed full accountability for performing at a high level, both quantitatively and qualitatively, and that they did this in the absence of a supervisory structure. The ALCS experience buttresses the soundness of the premise that mature practitioners can be relied upon to carry out their professional role and accountability for the quality of their service to clients—perhaps even more because they experience directly what is involved when full responsibility is vested in them. It also appears that the ALCS staff's response to accountability to the profession—in writing, sharing the results of studies or engaging in research—is related to the fact that such accountability in general, in the era of their education and socialization, was not defined or advocated academically, and was not encouraged by social agencies.

### 3. The Executive Director's Reactions

It is difficult to report the areas of readjustment required for the elimination of supervision and vesting accountability for quality of service in the practitioner. In self-observation there is always the danger of failing to note evidence of areas of concern not consciously perceived. I had anticipated that it would not be easy to relinquish accustomed work methods and habits that had been acquired over the years, despite my intellectual acceptance of the desirability of change. It was impossible, however, to foresee some problems that appeared later.

One such unanticipated difficulty arose in the area of the administrative process of monitoring—one of the responsibilities of any executive. This includes watching trends (whether in client expectations, client problems or theoretical advances for use in practice, and so on) for the purpose of being certain that an agency's program and policies are consistent with changes that are occurring either in the client community or in professional practice. But monitoring also includes noting whether policies and procedures are being observed by staff. The primary purpose is to discover in what areas revisions are necessary, but monitoring is also an element in the evaluation of practitioner performance.

I had no difficulty in accepting the fact that the professionals were accountable for the quality of their practice. Not to monitor them in this area required only my consciously controlling my former ways of relating to staff during an initial period in which they were learning and beginning to accept their new responsibilities. Undoubtedly this was because, in my previous professional experience as supervisor, subadministrator and administrator, I had had to develop a theory or rationale for how I carried out my responsibilities and toward what objective. In relation to the practice of staff, I had developed a concept of the supervisory role, what its objectives were, and what an administrator could or could not do to guarantee as high a caliber of practitioner performance as was possible. I had also had the opportunity to test out my ideas in previous positions. [104]    These convictions and hypotheses are apparent in the structure upon which ALCS was built. I was prepared for transitional problems that the staff might experience in taking on their new responsibilities for practice. I had foreseen to some extent what my role would be in building a milieu for a relationship that would help staff carry the newly defined responsibilities. I had the full support of the board, who also believed that social workers must eventually carry direct and complete accountability for the quality of their service. This undoubtedly was a large factor in the ease with which I could tolerate the initial testing out of the hypotheses and relinquish my former responsibility as a supervisor or administrator who feels continuously and directly accountable for the quality of agency service because of the various levels of competence represented in most agency staffs. Moreover, as staff assumed their responsibility, my conviction grew. They did rise to the demands that direct accountability put upon them, whether this was for additional education or the meeting of a client's needs, even at great personal inconvenience (for example, making home visits at night, or planning for being periodically in touch with a client during one's vacation). Whatever was necessary to be soundly helpful to a client was carried out by the practitioner. It is important to note that at no time did the staff give any evidence of needing my approval of them as responsible persons when they rose to unusual activity required by the needs of specific clients.

Despite this, I did have one area of concern which I was not able to control consciously and which did create strain between myself and the staff. This was the matter of currency in recording the "agency record." The staff had established the expectations about currency on the basis of what was considered essential for sound service. This included the needs of clients as well as what was helpful in the review of one's own practice in general and for the administration of the agency. [105] On this basis, we set up a system of clerical notification to professional staff when recording was due.

Staff reacted in characteristic fashion. A few kept their recording up to date. Occasionally all staff members met expectations after a brief lag of a self-granted time extension. At times several members of the group appeared to be ignoring the expectations. On these occasions, I took responsibility for calling staff attention to the discrepancy between standards they had set and their adherence to them, noting that such failure might mean that the expectations were unrealistic or that the policy should be reviewed by the total staff. Certainly this was one of my intents. The staff, however, quickly reacted to an additional unexpressed element in my action—that I was monitoring the individual practitioners who tended to ignore the policy. I was in effect substituting a group process disguised as a need to review policy, as a control over individual practitioners. Undoubtedly I did this to avoid a return to a former supervisory relationship in which the individual is asked to review the meaning of his failure to conform to policies. The group reacted as if I were monitoring all of them individually. Those who had ignored the expectations reacted as if I had set the expectations or was interpreting them rigidly. The others either defended their colleagues or were silent, obviously resenting my action as contradictory to their independent status.

The group's reaction and my rising anger made me examine the cause of tension. I took responsibility for discussing with the staff the inappropriateness of my continuing to monitor them and my having thus created and perpetuated an area of strain. I also discussed with them, however, my feeling that our seeming impasse could imply our actual concurrence in resisting change. I told them that I believed they either had to decide that recording was not essential or find some way of holding themselves accountable for meeting the expectations they themselves had set. This done, I could cease the inappropriate monitoring. The group then decided that when a practitioner failed to meet the deadline for recording, he would not schedule himself for intake appointments until his dictation was completed. The new policy was effective. While it could hardly be described as "internalization" of the value of recording (for client and agency), it did at least remove an area of tension between the staff and myself.

I can think of possible explanations for my persistence in monitoring the staff's failure to adhere to their own decisions on recording. Their action interfered with my own tasks, one of which was the periodic review of all closed cases (monitoring for program needs). Equally important is the fact that the content and purpose of case recording have never been clearly defined. Recording had its origins in meeting the anticipated demands of the donors to explain why help was or was not given in individual situations, as well as to indicate how much was given (costs). Records later became a means of first training apprentices, and then educating professionals. Recording content became more elaborate as social work began to integrate psychological and psychiatric understandings into client services. It was believed that social workers could not make diagnoses and that our function was to produce details from which consultants in psychiatry or agency supervisors could make diagnoses. Thus records became a form of justification for diagnostic and treatment decisions. We are still caught up in our past tradition and our recording practice reflects the concept that it is a form of evaluation of us in fulfilling the expectations of our employer. Therefore, I believe that the ALCS staff's behavior and mine were related in part to a general lack of conviction about the value of current types of recording for treatment.

Tension between me and the staff did not occur in another area, fee collection, in which there were also occasional lapses. The periodic clerical listing of fees owed and the last date of client contact, which was available to all staff, did occasionally indicate the possibility that a practitioner had not dealt with a client's failure to pay his bill. Yet in these instances I experienced no need to monitor the staff member. It is my opinion that this difference was related to the clarity staff had developed about the relationship of payment to treatment—something on which all of us were in agreement. A similar clarity had yet to be achieved for recording.

### Costs, Source of Income and Accountability

By now it is obvious that one of the major differences between ALCS and other social agencies was its source of income. Funding for the pilot demonstration was provided by a private philanthropy, but it was actually a grant to support an experiment. One element of the experiment was to work toward having the service program completely supported by client fees. These differences in the source of funding produced changes in the respective responsibilities of board, executive and staff for ensuring agency support and for accounting for the agency's costs.

In a philanthropic social agency, support from a donor group requires the agency to give a periodic accounting not only for the continued need for its program but also for how the money was spent and whether its clientele and the community received adequate value in return. In the philanthropic agency, the board of directors has been responsible for such accounting, a role established in the pre-professional era of social work when the board represented the donor group. The current trend is toward selecting as board members persons who represent the broader community. Nevertheless, the board is still considered to be the body accountable to the donor community although board members themselves are not as comfortable with this role as they were in the past. As agencies have become increasingly professional, supervisory and administrative staff members indirectly assume responsibility for accounting for agency costs; they advise the board, accompany board members to meetings with representatives of the donor group, and serve as resource persons, but they are not held directly accountable.

A pilot program such as ALCS is not subject to the same continuous review as is a service agency. Accountability to the donor for the costs of a pilot program has been fulfilled once the grant is made. Accountability for the *outcome* of the pilot program is owed not to the donor but to the profession.

In an agency that aims to become nonphilanthropic and hopes to depend wholly on its clients for support, the key issue is the client's response to the practitioner's competence. The client is the one who raises the questions about what he is receiving, how services are offered him and the costs of service. He does this within the professional interview. Whether or not he puts it in words, he is constantly assessing and setting the value of what he is receiving in return for what he is paying. This is true whether he complains about being charged an extra fee for an extended interview, refuses to accept a transfer to another worker, or expresses disappointment in the treatment he is receiving. The practitioner has to consider the meaning of the client's complaint or action. Is he expressing his expectations of how service should be offered him, of what service he requires? Are his expectations valid and consistent with sound service, or are they expressions of his core problems which brought him into treatment? Is his reaction a comment on the practitioner's competence and is his estimate correct? Or is it solely an expression of his general problems in relationship and in functioning? The practitioner's response represents his accountability to the client for quality and cost of service. That is, if the client's reactions are considered valid, the practitioner may initiate a review of policy or procedure, or he may seek consultation or additional education for himself. If the practitioner evaluates the responses as related to the client's core problems, he must deal with them within their therapeutic context. Therefore, it is through the practitioner staff and not the agency board that direct accountability to the client for the cost of treatment falls. Being accountable to the client requires full use of professional competence and, therefore, is a professional staff's responsibility and not a board's.

No one in ALCS was really prepared for the impact of the new source of support on the roles of board and staff in regard to accountability for costs, nor for its effect on the relationship between board and staff. The staff's previous experience in other social agencies had socialized them to being responsible employees, advising the board of the requirements for sound service and "educating" them. The ALCS board's previous experience had trained its members to be accountable for funding and costs of program. The relationship had been one in which the board made all final decisions, since most decisions involve fiscal considerations. The continued compartmentalization of major roles for professional staff and board and the relationship that is necessary under the circumstances left the ALCS board and staff uncomfortable—even more so as the agency became increasingly (and eventually totally) supported by fees earned.

The original pilot structure provides some glimpses of the partnership relationship that would eventually evolve. Partnership was implied in the invitation to serve on the board. The basis of their selection included both their substantial experience with and knowledge of social agencies, and their concurrence in the potential value to all social agencies and clients of public recognition of social work as a profession. The element of partnership was also implied in what was discussed with professional candidates in the hiring process. They were asked to weigh their own conviction of the value of the project for all agencies and clients, and to be ready to be accountable to the profession rather than to the board as their employer. All were undoubtedly so concerned with reaching their target clientele, however, that they were not fully aware that success could lead to changes in board and staff roles and relationships.

From the first, board members seemed aware of their altered role in relation to cost accountability. The questions

they raised individually with the Executive Director revealed their uncertainty and discomfort. They asked whether they were advisors and, if so, to whom. Were they advisors to the Lehman family?—a natural question because
several members of the family held office on the board.
Were they advisors to the professional staff? If so, in what
areas was their advice wanted? Were they responsible for
policy decisions, even though they were only asked to concur with staff recommendations? It would appear that some
board members were feeling detached from their accustomed base for making decisions. They had been used to
deciding what could be financially supported when the
professional staff made recommendations concerning essential programs and standards. At ALCS they did not
have to decide what would be supported by a donor community, since the original grant was open-ended. All decisions were to be made solely on the basis of what was
essential for high caliber service. This placed the board in
an *equal* role with professional staff in making decisions on
professional policies and issues. One board member, early
in the agency's history, reported that, in telling a group of
her friends that she had accepted service on the ALCS
board, she had been startled to realize for the first time
that she was backing a professional service rather than
sponsoring a means of easing the lot of the poor! It had
made her ask herself what she knew about social work,
whether she did believe it was a profession of value to
persons in all walks of life, and what her contribution
could be in an agency like ALCS. She became quite excited
when she realized that board and staff now could work together in deciding what sound service required since no fiscal problem was involved. The potentialities of a partnership had occurred to her. She was not alone in her initial
quandary. Other board members raised similar questions
about ALCS's need for a board. Several members believed

they did have a role but it should be more specifically stated to distinguish it from the usual board role. They also believed that the criteria for board selection should be re-examined. Since they were not needed as representatives of the donor community, should they be more represent-ative of the client group or of the profession? Some board members thought they would be essential only until licens-ing had been secured.

In one area the board maintained conviction about its traditional role—deciding on the salaries to be paid and the guidelines to be used for increases. The one exception was the board's acceptance of the Executive Director's recom-mendation for the initial salary in 1954. The board also assumed responsibility for fee-setting, but this did not cre-ate the same tension between them and the staff. Yet the board members were not entirely comfortable with their role in salary determination, if a retrospective interpretation of some of their comments and reactions is correct. They frequently requested an executive canvass of staff opinions concerning salaries and they provided a means of the staff's earning more through sharing the increased income from fees. They also suggested that the staff participate in board meetings, yet they were reluctant to have them present if financial matters or salaries were to be discussed. In brief, they felt their relationship to ALCS staff should be dif-ferent, but were uncertain where changes should occur.

The staff had no apparent discomfort in assuming part of the responsibility for determining costs—for example, in setting interview production standards. They were not willing, however, to take a similar responsibility for helping to determine salaries. They did not see the need for their being concerned with how the income to pay salaries could be secured. Even after 1957, when there was every indica-tion that the agency could be supported on fees, the staff complained about what they were paid. They did not respond to the Executive Director's suggestion that the various alternatives be considered for increasing income and making higher salaries possible, and that the board should be informed of the executive and staff recommendations. They still saw salary determination as the responsibility of the board, despite their own stated commitment to a self-supporting program.

This situation placed the Executive Director in an uncomfortable role as a channel of communication between board and staff on the issue of salary, particularly after 1957. She agreed with the staff that the traditional guide lines for social agency salaries were inappropriate in an agency supported by client fees, yet was ineffective in persuading the board to see the "marketplace" as providing guidelines for salary determination. She was also ineffective in helping the staff recognize that more than their wishes had to be considered in setting salaries in an agency committed to self-support. The Executive Director believed that the staff had as much right to set their salaries as did the board, but also had equal responsibility for assuring the fiscal soundness of the agency. They could not ignore this fact if indeed they wished to have either a group practice or a social agency structure to serve the financially advantaged clients.

In considering the divergence in points of view and her inability to bring about a reconciliation, the Executive Director and the President of the board decided that it was essential to have some direct communication between the board and the staff, so that they could recognize their mutual responsibilities and objectives and begin to deal with them. It was at this point that agreement was reached to have all agency committees composed of both board and staff; no one was to serve as a representative of a particular group, but as an individual working with others to arrive at recommendations for board action. All were aware that if the expectation of these committees were to be realized, there would be need to consider later the possibility of staff participation both on the board's Administrative Committee and in board meetings. The more cautious step was taken because of the legal regulations requiring that nonprofit organization staff have no voice in the final decisions on salaries.

Of all the committees appointed after 1962 the Finance Committee was the most pertinent to accountability for costs. It was also the most crucial committee, insofar as a partnership relationship between board and staff was concerned. The questions of salary and personnel costs that would come to this committee would be a real test of whether board and staff could focus on a common objective. Could they give up vested interests, either as persons who wished to earn more money or as persons who wished to keep the costs of service down? [106] Could they keep their focus on a sound fiscal policy essential for high quality service to clients as well as for agency continuity? Could they see that planning for the sound fiscal management of the agency was a mutual interest?

As reported earlier, after a period of clarification that their relationship was not one of negotiation, the members of the Finance Committee were able to focus on the objective of a sound fiscal base for the agency. A true partnership in the provision of a needed service did come about. This direct interplay helped board and staff alike to see that they were equally committed to self-support and to a high caliber of service to clients. Each member of the group developed respect for the special knowledge and competence of the other. Those members who were selected from the board could see that the staff was capable of realistic financial planning when given the opportunity to do it; and the staff began to respect the board's interest in seeing that staff received adequate compensation. Fiscal briefing occurred simultaneously for all members of the Finance Committee. All showed an equal interest in understanding the meaning of the various points made about fiscal matters and benefited from each other's questions.

The experience of serving on the Finance Committee convinced the staff that an essential component of mature professional practice is an ability to understand and be accountable for costs of service. They recognized that preparation for a similar role in a philanthropic agency would involve factors other than those present at ALCS. Nevertheless, they believed that just as practitioners are prepared for their eventual accountability for quality of service, they should be prepared for their eventual accountability for the use of funds supplied by the public. How this could be achieved posed an interesting problem.

In retrospect, one might ask why the board and staff accepted the executive's initial recommendation on salary. Why was there no apparent difficulty with the later decision that ALCS salary would be competitive with salaries of comparable workers in other social agencies? Perhaps this was because in the early years ALCS was looked upon as a temporary agency. By and large, the staff expected to return to other social agencies once the experiment was completed. The initial recommendation and the board's subsequent assurance that salaries would remain competitive with those of social agencies did not challenge the traditional and established guidelines to which board and staff alike were accustomed.

It was when the pilot phase was completed and income from fees was substantial that tension developed between board and staff over the issue of salaries. The need for service to the clientele had been established. It seemed feasible for the agency to think of becoming permanent, particularly since there was no apparent movement on the part of New York City's family agencies to extend their services to the ALCS target clientele. With the decision to continue the agency and in view of the staff's role in ensuring income, it was natural for them to grow restless and to begin comparing their salaries with those of private practitioners. In so doing, they were challenging the traditional board guidelines for salary determination. (The executive's own belief that it was the client who would ultimately determine salaries by what he was willing to pay for service received was also a challenge to tradition.) The staff's refusal (up to 1965) to accept responsibility for determining the salary and how it could be achieved was evidence that they were still acting as *employees*, not as *partners* who should share responsibility in deciding how the costs of service could be met. After 1965, with the change in structure of the Finance Committee, a relationship of partners began to emerge.

It now seems that one important factor in the board members' adhering to their traditional role in the matter of salaries, despite their discomfort, was their continued membership on boards of other social agencies, where they had to be concerned with securing sufficient income to meet increasing costs and salary demands. It was probably difficult for them to try to explain to those agencies (let alone to their unions) the relationship between the source of support of ALCS and its staff salaries, in contrast with the source of support of a philanthropic agency.

The ALCS experience highlights the effect on both professionals and board members of being socialized to their traditional roles in a philanthropic system. The board had been socialized to fill the role of providers who were expert in securing funds and in monitoring and accounting for their use. The staff had been socialized to the role of serving clients within defined programs and policies, but not to the role of financial planners. Over the years boards have increasingly accepted the unreality of separating funding from quality of service; yet boards and staffs continue to function as if it were possible to have such a separation and therefore to assign distinct and separate roles to the two groups. This may account for the phenomenon ALCS experienced in the board's total acceptance of the staff recommendations concerning such cost factors as the number of interviews and their simultaneous inability to accept a similar staff role in salary determination. It may account also for the professionals' ambivalence in accepting total responsibility for service costs in some areas and their refusal to share responsibility for finding the means for paying their salaries.

In an agency supported on fees earned by staff through service to clients, a partnership relationship between board and staff is indeed essential. The philanthropic agency, dependent as it is on various sources of support and acting as a training center for staff and board members, may find a similar relationship difficult to achieve. Nevertheless, it is a goal toward which, it is to be hoped, all board and staff members should be socialized to prepare them for their eventual collaboration in the provision of sound community services.

## Other Findings

Two other matters, both related to the issue of accountability, deserve comment: the policy on sick leave and the stability of staff. The Technical Advisory Committee believed that the ALCS experience in these areas would be of interest to other social agencies and urged including it in the report.

### 1. Sick Leave

The sick leave policy, setting no time limitations, was unique for a social agency. Established initially with only the professional staff in mind, it also covered the clerical staff until an incident in 1967 motivated a clarification of the policy because of the difference in accountability of professionals and clerical employees.

On the average, the professional staff took 1.24 days of sick leave a year, over the entire 15½ years—a remarkably small number. The clerical staff averaged 3.6 days a year—again, a modest number. In one year the latter average rose markedly because of the illness of one clerical worker, who eventually required serious surgery. On the whole, however, the amount of time lost to sick leave was minimal, attesting to good morale and dedication.

The mature professional person's concern for his client is surely a factor in his decision to come to work if at all possible, even when he is ill. He takes into account the effect on certain clients of his absence, and the overriding importance of the client's need for help. The professional staff's identification with the goal of agency support through fees was undoubtedly another factor. It is also possible that the policy itself seemed fair and considerate and thus did not create a temptation to abuse it. But it would seem that the primary factor was the integrity of the staff's commitment to their clients and their professional stance in relation to accountability to clients and to overall agency objectives.

The clerical staff's adherence to the intent of the policy may have been in part related to the quality of persons selected. They were as interested in the goals of ALCS (especially during the pilot years) as were professional staff. Sick leave policy and the responsibilities they carried in its appropriate use were discussed with them at the point of hiring. They understood the relation between abusing the policy and increasing agency costs, which also meant increasing the workload of the professional staff. They were proud of the professional staff's competence, even when the work habits or idiosyncracies of some practitioners

irritated them. In addition, deviations from expected behavior, when they occurred, were dealt with promptly. In
only one instance was it necessary to dismiss a receptionist
because of her abuse of sick leave.

### 2. Stability of Staff

It is difficult to describe stability of staff in an agency
that had no history before 1954 and added staff only as
need arose and qualified persons could be obtained. However, it may be useful to state that a total of eighteen
persons were hired as members of the regular staff during
the 15½ years. Of this number, seven were still on the staff
when ALCS transferred the client service program to the
Park East Counseling Group (January 1, 1970), and had
been in the agency anywhere from three-quarters of a year
to 13¾ years. (See list of staff in Appendix.)

Of the eleven practitioners who left the agency before
December, 1969, two had gone in response to their family's
needs that took them out of the city. These did not seek
work at first. Eventually they did secure positions in social
agency settings as practitioners. Four others left to take
subadministrative positions as, for example, case consultants. The remaining five left to enter private practice, either
on a full- or part-time basis.

Similarly, the evening, or part-time, staff remained fairly
stable. The first group eventually consisted of three men
and two women. [107]  By January 1, 1970, two of the
men were still with ALCS, one having served 10½ years, the
other 12½ years. Those who had left before that date had
served from 3½ years to 12½ years.

Another part-time person, on sabbatical leave from her
agency, had come to ALCS in June, 1956, to carry out a
part-time summer assignment. When her leave was over, she
returned to her former position but continued as a part-time
staff member at ALCS. She was still at ALCS at the time

of the transfer of the client program, having served for a period of 13½ years.

It would be difficult at this time to secure objective data to account for the stability of both the regular and the part-time staff. The Technical Advisory Committee has stated that one reason seemed to be the "achievement of staff partnership" in the financial structure of the agency. The members of the regular staff have expressed their own opinion that the sense of partnership was related to the total structure as conceived and administered. The milieu conveyed a sense of respect for them as professionals and for their integrity—an essential ingredient for collaboration or partnership. The staff did not feel that financial remuneration was a primary factor in their remaining with the organization. Rather, the primary factors were: 1) the opportunity provided for carrying responsibility as persons fully accountable for all aspects of professional service, and 2) their increasing role in the funding of the agency and their sense of participating with the board in a program that had potential values for the profession. Moreover, 3) they particularly valued the group practice, which gave them easy access to consultation in emergencies, coverage of their practice during illnesses or vacations, and the stimulation from the exchange with their peers of ideas on professional issues.

The stability of the evening staff may have been related to the opportunity provided for independent practice and a group process of consultation and exchange with a peer group. Most of those in the evening group were interested in the experimental and innovative aspects of the agency's structure since they held full-time positions as administrators, subexecutives, or supervisors. In fact, some of them did adapt features of the ALCS structure to their own agencies, in relation both to fee-setting and to defining the role of senior casework staff. [108]

# 5. *Termination of the ALCS Venture*

IN SEPTEMBER, 1968, the Executive Director asked to be relieved of her responsibilities by January 1, 1970. The President of the board, in keeping with the principle of board-staff collaboration, invited five members from each group to serve on a Planning Committee, with the charge to consider the future of ALCS and to make a recommendation to the board for the continuation of the service to clients.

The committee had some difficulty getting under way, primarily because the staff partially returned to a stance of negotiation with the board. They insisted that, rather than having the designated staff members accept the President's invitation to serve on the Planning Committee, they would elect the persons they wanted as their representatives. At the point of crisis, the staff apparently did not have the same confidence in their strength in a collaborative process as they had in their collective bargaining ability. Once their request concerning the selection of members on the Planning Committee was accepted, joint work was pursued, agreements were reached, and a plan for board consideration was mutually formulated.

One must recall that the board members were the same ones who had agreed initially to serve for a five- to ten-year period while a pilot program was undertaken. In the last

**151**

seven years, although engaged in building a new type of social agency, they had constantly raised questions about the need for the Board of Directors in an agency supported by client fees and manned by an experienced staff. Some were restless because they had stayed beyond their initial commitment. But their questions were concerned primarily with the agency structure needed. Had ALCS continued, there undoubtedly would have been a redefinition of board member qualifications as well as turnover in the board membership.

The Planning Committee considered several possibilities, one of which was to disband the agency, since it had achieved its pilot goals, letting the practitioners arrange to serve their remaining clients on a private basis. This suggestion was not favored by the committee, which viewed an *agency* resource as essential for the ALCS client group as well as valuable for the professional staff. A second alternative considered by the Planning Committee was to hire a new executive to carry on the work of further defining a new model of service delivery for upper-income clients. To do this would involve defining the responsibilities of the new executive, determining the qualifications essential and engaging in a search for a qualified person. Again, this proposal was not favorably received. In retrospect, it appears that the staff were not confident of exerting sufficient control over the selection of a new executive to assure that executive-staff collaboration would continue. Staff reactions to the Executive Director's resignation (and the time limit involved) prevented her helping staff to clarify the reason for their unfavorable reaction to this plan and to evaluate it. At the same time, the board members on the committee were reluctant to continue the responsibility of administering yet another social agency. A third possibility considered was to have ALCS become the "private pavilion" for the major family agencies in New York City.

Earlier, the Executive Director had explored the feasibility of this idea with individual members of the Technical Advisory Committee, presenting no explicit plan but merely suggesting that as one possibility each agency might ask a few members of its board to represent the agency on a joint board to administer ALCS. At that time, it had been assumed that the Executive Director would remain. When this question was reopened at the time of the request to resign, individual members of the Technical Advisory Committee responded as they had previously: they believed that the various family agencies had too many differences in personnel practices and concepts of how service was best provided to make a joint private pavilion possible. Members of ALCS staff were not in favor of the plan because they saw this as a return to their traditional roles in family agencies—roles no longer acceptable to them—and they prized their professional responsibility for agency self-support.

The plan most favored by the Planning Committee was one that the Executive Director had also explored earlier with a few schools of social work in the New York area: that ALCS become an integral part of a school of social work to test the idea that such a school and a social agency could have a relationship similar to that between a hospital and a medical school. Earlier discussions with schools had indicated an interest in the idea, particularly if funding could be secured. It was seen as an excellent avenue for exchange between social work practitioners and educators, which might result in their collaborating in the formulation of curriculum, course content, and educational materials. Because ALCS in 1968 was a self-supporting unit with a contingency fund, the question of financing was not a deterrent. However, other circumstances within the schools (1968-69) made such an affiliation impossible. Two schools, for example, were seeking new deans and therefore were not in a position to consider the plan for at least one or two years. One school had ideas for a similar plan, namely to set up an agency to serve its immediate community. One school frankly expressed concern about serving an upper-income group in the light of the general concern with lack of services for the poor.

Although the entire staff preferred the plan of the agency's affiliating with a school, they were aware that it might not be feasible. Therefore, they presented the Planning Committee with their decision to continue as a group practice unit whether or not the board concurred. For the latter, a plan for continuity of the agency beyond the individual interests of the seven remaining staff was essential. Also, the board asked that the group establish a tie with the social work profession. These conditions were really the result of an earlier exploration by staff, at the board's request, concerning the values in a group practice, as well as their own interest in such a plan for themselves as the "inheritors" of the client service program after the pilot goal had been achieved. The request and invitation were later withdrawn on the advice of the Technical Advisory Committee, who believed that a group practice without board aegis would not assure continuity of the resource, and that a contribution to the profession of social work would not be one of group self-expectations.

In the plan submitted to the Planning Committee by the staff, a method for assuring continuity of the agency was included. Several alternatives for a link between the agency and the profession (liaison with a school of social work, an advisory committee of leading social workers) were being explored. The Planning Committee, therefore, recommended to the board that the program of service to clients be transferred to the staff as of January 1, 1970. The staff formed a group practice, adopted a new name and worked out the basic features of their joint venture. The board gave support to this move in three ways: for a two-year period, allowing the group to identify the new group practice with the service formerly offered by ALCS; giving the group a loan to help cover initial operating expenses, with a special arrangement to assure continuity of service to clients transferred to them for a period of two years [109]; and signing a joint letter announcing the termination of the client service program by ALCS and its transfer to the Park East Counseling Group. By January 1, 1970, the Park East Counseling Group was officially established. ALCS continued as an entity only for the purpose of completing its report to the profession and terminating its research commitment responsibly.

# 6. Implications for Voluntary Agencies and Social Work

*Structure and Goals.* Perhaps the most significant insight for those who worked at ALCS and perhaps will be for those in other social agencies is in the degree to which social agencies have clung to the structure that had been conceived in the preprofessional era of social work and had logic then. The fact was that the structure had become less and less viable and logical with time and the changes (which should have influenced the structure of the social agency) were handled by accommodations to the structure. These reduced excessive strain and made it possible to operate within the given structure. They did not necessarily however, resolve the problem or answer the issue from which the strain emerged. ALCS provided an unusual professional opportunity—that of beginning a new social agency based on somewhat different concepts—forcing an analysis of the structure needed to achieve the stated goals. ALCS was to reach a clientele needing but not using the services of a social agency. It was assumed that they would expect and certainly could afford to pay full cost of service, and in return would expect to have the help of fully competent, experienced professional practitioners. These facts meant, for example, that a social agency must be designed in a way that would be nonphilanthropic in its source of funding and, therefore, would be unique in 1954.

The staff must have the fullest professional competence possible in social work at that time, and this competence would need to be recognized in the respective agency staff roles. In addition, this meeting of the client's expectations would actually give him an unusual role in determining the agency design.

The ALCS experience suggests that it is not only timely but urgent as well for all voluntary social agencies consciously to review their structure.

*What units do their agencies now have?*

*How have their roles and responsibilities been defined?*

*What is the nature of their relationship to each other?*

*What are the channels of communication established among and between them?*

*Who is currently carrying the agency's accountability to the source of financial support, to the clients they serve, to the profession of social work?*

*Do these people have the necessary competence and knowledge and are they in a position of trust within the community to whom they are accountable?*

These are a few of the questions which, if consciously and objectively reviewed, will undoubtedly lead to a number of hypotheses about potential realignment and resolutions of tensions that all agencies are currently experiencing. If a number of hypotheses are tested out by agencies, a more viable structure may emerge, taking into account the demands of an ever-changing milieu in which the voluntary social agency operates.

It is the purpose of this chapter to raise the issues and to present some answers which were tested at ALCS. We have noted that there have been major changes in the milieu in which the social agency functions since its origins in the preprofessional era. Three of these changes bear review.

*Funding.* The first major change is in the funding of the

social agency. In the preprofessional era the source of the voluntary agency's funding was a relatively small, somewhat homogeneous socioeconomic group of contributors. Because there was no profession, it was the contributor who determined what was to be provided and for whom. In structuring an agency to carry out the program, the donor group envisioned the need for two units in a social agency: a board of directors and a staff. The board of directors, drawn from the donor group, assumed the responsibility of implementing the consensus of the group. They made all final policy decisions regarding the services that would be offered, and the procedures for rendering those services. They were expected to direct the staff. Over the years, as new agencies have been set up and boards have been selected and appointed, they have been prepared to assume the same responsibilities: using funds to achieve the purpose of the donor group; accounting to that group for use of the funds; explaining to the donors why additional funding might be needed or why new programs should be devised; and having final authority in shaping agency policies.

Strain in carrying this role undoubtedly arose as soon as the complexity of achieving an agency's goals became apparent. The staff, as employees, made boards of directors aware of the relationship between what and how they were providing and achieving their aims. Board members came to respect the knowledge of staff and, as a result, found themselves in the role of interpreters and mediators between the larger donor group and their employees. This role of mediator was an accommodation to the beginning development of professional knowledge within the employee group.

Role tensions for boards have continued and been magnified with the ever-increasing professional character of social work. Boards realize that costs of service are closely interwoven with the quality of service; but it is not easy for a board to have to rely heavily on the professional staff for understanding what quality of service entails and to defend it with lay groups. It creates problems for the professional person as well and often strains the relationship between staff and board.

Another source of tension for the board has been the considerably broadened source of financial support. Many agencies derive a substantial portion of their funds by allocation from United Funds or Federations, whose contributors have become increasingly representative of all socioeconomic groups in the community rather than confined to a handful of large donors. As a result, some members of boards have questioned whether they are truly representative of the total donor community.

In addition, there are new, impersonal sources of income, of which the governmental subsidy to the voluntary social agency is one. Such a subsidy is given if an agency is willing to *provide the services defined by legislation within the standards and expectations set by the government.* Another derives from the growing practice of health insurance plans to include social service departments of hospitals and voluntary social agencies as vendors of social services. *The vendor can be reimbursed for his service if he has met the insurer's standards and expectations.* ALCS has proved the viability of a third source of funding—*the client who can pay a fee set by the agency which covers full cost of service.* This client also has his expectations and standards that must be met if he is to use the service and continue to be a source of income. [110]

When the funding source is governmental, an insurer or a client paying full cost of service, the mediating role of the board is no longer viable. To be a mediator one must have direct contact with each of the respective groups, a virtual impossibility. The relationship of the social agency to these new sources of support must be consciously reviewed to see how one can influence governmental or insurer groups to meet the particular needs of specific communities. In such a review it will not only be necessary to consider methods for reaching and influencing these sources of income, but also to ensure that whoever is selected to reach and influence these sources must have knowledge, competence and trust if he is to fulfill his agency role. In relation to the client who pays full cost of service, the ALCS experience suggests that the board can have no direct role in accountability. This needs to be carried by the practitioner, requiring specialized preparation and experience to understand the administrative significance of the client's questions related to accountability as well as the therapeutic questions that might be involved.

*Professionalization of Social Work.* A second change that has occurred in the milieu of the voluntary social agency has been the increasing professional character of social work. Originally the social worker had been socialized toward fulfilling the role of employee accountable to a board of directors as employers. Strain in carrying this role probably began with the social worker's initial acquisition of practice wisdom, important for the effective carrying out of the intent of the donor group. The beginning sense of professional knowledge and competence brought with it a feeling of accountability to the client. The social worker made an accommodation to this growing sense of professional role by "educating" the board and keeping his employer informed. Although the strain may have been more or less diminished by this accommodation, it did permit the continuance of an agency structure in which the board makes the final policy decisions and the social worker is ultimately accountable to the board for carrying out its direction.

*Accountability.* The difference has been sharpened between the accountability of a practitioner with "employee" status and that of an acknowledged professional. The former is hired to carry out assigned tasks within the limits of the employer's policies and procedures. Since he is expected to carry out his tasks intelligently, he will be functioning responsibly if he keeps his employer informed of how the latter's directions, policies and procedures affect the achievement of his own goals and intent. The responsible employee keeps his employer informed about the changes he believes should be made and the additional services he believes are needed, and supports these suggestions with facts. His accountability ends, however, when he has submitted this information to his employer; he is not responsible for what the employer does with his recommendations. He may feel frustrated. He may see his employer as defeating his own purposes. He may feel pride in the fact that he has contributed toward the improvement of the program when his recommendations are accepted. But as an employee he can be only indirectly accountable to his client through the use of his influence and his ability to educate and persuade his employer. Even within this role he is limited because he has little occasion to learn or understand fiscal management and funding.

By contrast, the professional practitioner is primarily accountable to his clients, current and potential. He cannot avoid his responsibility for the quality of service he offers, whether given on his own as in private practice, or in conjunction with others as in a social agency. In social work, there has been an ever-increasing expectation within the profession that the individual practitioner will be more directly involved in his accountability to his client. [111] To do this, however, it will be necessary for the agency to be altered so that he can, from his beginning experience as a student, be more and more involved in the agency's total accountability, that is, not only for quality of service but also for use of funds and for quantity of service. To carry this kind of role, he will also need to have a broader orienting knowledge base for his practice, one that includes information on funding as well as some opportunity for involvement in the processes of administrative decision making.

*Client Concept and Role.* The third change that has occurred and is still occurring is in the concept of the client. The original purpose of the voluntary social agency was to provide assistance in one form or another to the poor. Its purpose was philanthropic and expressed the conscience of the donors toward persons in their own community who were less fortunate economically. Later it became apparent that, to provide effective whole-person assistance, agencies must recognize clients' psychological needs. [112] Counseling and psychotherapeutic services, at first offered in connection with the use of "concrete" services, eventually became services in themselves. However, the social agency retained its philanthropic purpose and such services are still being offered to the economically less advantaged only. (While this statement may be challenged by many voluntary agencies, the fact remains that the ALCS experience indicates that a large number of middle- and upper-income groups will use the agency's services *only* if they are offered to them under certain conditions. The fact that agencies do not do so unconditionally constitutes a barrier to broader use of the social agency.)

Today the social agency's philanthropic purpose is being challenged within the social work profession and by some clients. This began with the advent of the governmental social agency, with the issue of whether their services were based on philanthropy or on the rights of citizens in a democracy. The latter concept is based on the conviction that all persons have identical human needs regardless of socioeconomic status and that a variety of services is required to meet these needs. The socioeconomic status may determine which type of social service the client needs, whether this will be primarily economic, for example, or not. However, in a democratic society, provision to meet these needs has come to be recognized as a matter of rights of citizens. The issue has been more militantly undertaken in recent years with a number of social workers and many clients demanding that clients have a voice in the voluntary agency's program and its policies.

The future structure of the social agency will certainly depend on which of these views gains ascendancy. What changes will be required cannot be fully foreseen. They will become clear only when the purpose of a social agency is more clearly established by lay and professional leaders and is accepted by the public in general. Under the philanthropic view of the voluntary social agency, the client is solely the recipient of help. He is given no direct role in shaping the agency's program or policies and his social worker is his channel for expressing his expectations. The donor views the client as a person worthy of concern, someone in need of defense and of assistance, but with a limited role, however, because he is the recipient of charitable dollars. Under the concept of a social agency as responsible for seeing that citizen rights are ensured, the client is viewed as entitled to a participatory role in shaping the program and the services he needs.

Today board members and social workers alike are uncomfortable with the lack of a defined and direct role for the client. They agree that he should participate in developing the agency's program and policies, but they are not certain how best to accomplish this. Opening the door to clients as members of the board or to a client group as a new component unit of the agency presents new problems for both board members and staff. The board member undoubtedly is concerned about whether the client will accept the fact that funds are limited, and whether as a power group clients will "exploit" the philanthropically-minded community. Boards may even question whether clients hold the same economic philosophy that they espouse. And professional staff undoubtedly fear that the introduction of the client group will create further problems for them in maintaining the necessary professional preparation through education. Agencies that have included clients as board members have reported varying and inconclusive experiences in attempting to meet this need.

ALCS, too, faced the question of an appropriate role for the client, his voice in the agency's program and its general administration. On several occasions consideration was given to adding former clients to the board, but no such decision was made. At first perhaps this was out of general discomfort with what felt like a radical idea, or perhaps because the board members did represent the clients' socioeconomic group. However, with accumulated experience, ALCS saw that the client was actually in a position of power, having a strong voice as the sole source of the agency's income and hence its survival. One has but to review the sections of this report dealing with the expansion of the program of services, the development of a continuing staff educational program, the revision of personnel practices, of changes in procedures, to see the impact of the client's expectations upon the various aspects of the agency's life. [113] The financial freedom of our client to seek help from other professional resources in New York City was his source of strength. He was in the same position that any source of significant financial support has in relation to a voluntary social agency. However, as a source of support the ALCS client seemed more attuned to the profession's explanations of the demands of sound service than can be said of most other sources of support. The direct experience of being helped was an important ingredient in the client's responsiveness to explanations, when these were valid. (The term "seemed" is used advisedly since no research on this issue was done.)

*Agency as Vendor.* The significance for others of the ALCS experience lies in the potential role offered clients of voluntary social agencies in the development of the vendor system. The client's freedom to choose his vendor puts him in a position of power similar to that of any source of income in influencing various aspects of an agency's life. However, the success of the vendor system will depend upon two factors at least. The client must have access to more than one resource for help. The second will be in the rapidity with which social agencies recognize that the practitioner's direct accountability to the client will require that he see himself as accountable not only for quality of his service but also for quantity and costs of service. The point has been made earlier that costs and quality are indivisible, and that their separation is unrealistic and certainly not in keeping with professional expectations of each practitioner. Thus to carry out full accountability the practitioner must become informed in areas that normally have been largely confined to administrators and boards. The practitioner will need to understand all factors that enter into administrative decisions—funding, costing, management, policy making, community attitudes, and so forth—as well as the demands imposed in providing sound qualitative services. More than an intellectual orientation to such knowledge will be required if the vendor system is to be effective. The practitioner will be assuming a portion of the administrative role in his direct accountability to the client and therefore must understand this role more fully than has been true in the past.

*New Structure, New Roles.* If the vendor status for voluntary agencies becomes a major source of income, then the current structure and its division of roles assigned to board and staff will change. However, whether this occurs or not, it is timely to examine in particular current roles and responsibilities assigned units of the voluntary social agency and the relationship that exists, toward which each is socialized.

*Does the current pattern take into account the closely interwoven character of costs, funding adequacy and quality of program and service rendered?*

*Does the current definition of role permit the professional to carry out his full accountability to his client?*

*Is it possible in the current system of division of tasks for lay and professional persons alike to develop the competence needed to carry out their functions? Are these functions correctly allocated and is the relationship of board-employer, staff-employee correct?*

ALCS was testing the hypothesis that a collaborative relationship between board and staff was more appropriate in view of current professional knowledge and the changed and varied sources of support. The details of what is meant by this collaborative relationship have been spelled out in earlier chapters. However, it may be well to highlight a few points. In a collaborative relationship, board and professional staff are equally committed to the provision of services to meet a specific community need. Everyone who enters to some extent chooses the agency as the locus of his work—lay or professional—out of a particular interest in the program itself. [114]   The essential difference between a collaborative and participatory relationship of staff to board is in the decision-making processes and not necessarily in who does what. The difference also lies in the preparation for role of lay and professional persons so that they are socialized to collaborative roles. For example, practitioners will carry the direct role of giving service to clients. However, decisions regarding policies that determine what can be offered and under what conditions will need to be made jointly.

*Educational Implications.* It can be argued that this is true today because all final decisions are made by top administrative professional personnel and board, though the latter carries final authority. The relationship between top administration and board is informal and exchange does take place. However, board and professional persons are socialized towards an employer-employee status and with staff in an advisory, participatory role. This model, derived from industry, is now anachronistic. [115] The collaborative relationship requires that the practitioner from his earliest professional preparation become thoroughly familiar with all aspects of *agency* accountability—funding, costs, extension of programs, etc.—as well as his *professional* accountability to client and profession. Similarly the lay person would need to be informed on all aspects of agency accountability. One objective of the educational preparation for each would be an intelligent, informed and creative role as catalyst to the other. (The second would be to carry out specific functions.) To achieve this, the structure of the agency would need revision to provide direct contacts among all levels of experienced professional staff and similar levels of experienced board members, perhaps on committees charged with developing recommendations for another group to make final decisions. Such a final group should also assure that professional and board members have equal voice and vote in the decision-making process. The value of a collaborative board and professional relationship is that it places the professional in a direct and equal role for making decisions with the board. This may serve to help professional persons learn to validate requests or professional standards. It is anticipated that the collaborative role will require that practitioners develop competence in validation and that agency budgets include costs of studies and research as a part of the daily life and practice of staff.

The collaborative relationship offers the professional practitioner an opportunity to exercise his role in accountability. It places him in a position where he can become aware of the limitations of funding and of society's willingness to provide; this, in turn, enables him to apply his professional knowledge realistically in selecting the most viable of the possible resolutions of any conflict between clients' needs and funds available. It is a responsibility which no professional practitioner can avoid. For the board member, the collaborative role also places him in a logical position in relation to provision of services. In this relationship the informed board member can serve as catalyst to the professionals in clarification of standards needed, in validation of hypotheses upon which program and services are built, and even upon the values, ethics and knowledge of the profession. The success of his role as catalyst may influence his confidence in the profession and its services and in his ability to help provide needed funds.

In summary, the collaborative view of the relationship between professional staff and lay board in the voluntary social agency shifts the various aspects of the agency's accountability to the professional group, and places the board member in his rightful role of a concerned citizen ready to help provide financially for services whose validity can be increasingly attested to within a framework of clear standards for sound service.

# NOTES

1. As used here, the word "pilot" has the meaning of a "trial unit in experimentation or in testing apparatus or in checking techniques or costs preparatory to full scale activity." *Webster's Third New International Dictionary* (Springfield, Mass.: G. & C. Merriam Co., 1966).

2. Ira M. Younker, "Family Service: The Road Ahead," *Family Service Highlights,* 28:8 (October 1957).

3. See Appendix 1 for the names of the founding group.

4. See Ira M. Younker, "Casework: Profession or By-Product?", *Family Service Highlights* 14:2 (March 1953), for a clear presentation of the goal of the founding core of ALCS.

5. The Consultation Center of Jewish Family Service of New York was designed by Frances Taussig, executive director of the agency, and Ira M. Younker, a member of the board. Mrs. Frances L. Beatman, assistant director of the agency, and Sonia Penn, supervisor of the Consultation Center, contributed considerably to the program and its implementation. The Center was closed as a separate unit after five years, since its program was integrated into all district offices of the agency.

6. Alice D. Taggart, Sidney J. Berkowitz, and Sonia Penn, *Fee-Charging in a Family Agency* (New York: Family Service Association of America, 1944); Sidney J. Berkowitz, "Reactions of Clients and Caseworkers Toward Fees," *The Family Journal of Social Casework,* XXVII:4 (April 1947); Frances Levenson Beatman, "Interpretation of Agency Policy to Workers, Clients, Agency Board and Community," presented at National Conference on Social Welfare, May 15, 1951; Celia Brody, "Fee-Charging—A Dynamic in the Casework Process," *The Family Journal of Social Casework,* XXX:2

(February 1949); Marjorie Boggs, "The Administrative and Casework Aspects of Fee-Charging," *The Family Journal of Social Casework,* XXX:8 (October 1949); Tina Claire Jacobs, "Attitudes of Social Workers Toward Fees," *Social Casework,* XXXIII:5 (May 1952); Frederika Neumann, "Administrative and Community Implications of Fee-Charging," *Social Casework,* XXXIII:7 (July 1952). These articles are but a few of the early articles discussing the impact of fees on clients, caseworkers and agencies, and on treatment.

7.    There is evidence of the emergence of the private practice of social work as early as the 1920s. In 1921, the Philadelphia Chapter of the professional association (now NASW) wrote a letter to the national office raising questions about practicing social work on a private basis.

8.    The term *administrative structure* as used in this report refers to the component units of the agency, the assigned roles and responsibilities of each unit and the channels of communication within and between units.

9.    During the first six months, the Executive Director was the only staff member. Subsequently, as staff grew, recommendations were made by the group as a whole. Therefore, when the term *staff* is used, it may represent anywhere from one to eight persons.

10.    A discussion of "regular" staff appears later in this chapter under *3. The Casework Staff.*

11.    An "evening or part-time" staff was employed, beginning in 1957, to carry direct practice only. Initially it was seen as a means of adding men counselors to our practitioner staff. The "culture" of social work in 1954 (and to some extent even today) dictated that able male practitioners move into supervisory or administrative positions; direct practice was the first rung on the social work career ladder. Although the category of senior caseworker had begun to emerge at about this time, men were reluctant to accept such positions even when they might have preferred to do so. The supervisory and administrative positions held the connotation of advanced competence and status and were viewed as more likely to lead to higher salaries. This "cultural" aspect was in direct contrast to that of psychology, where clinical practice or direct service was considered the top rung of the career ladder, carrying connotations of advanced competence and status.

Our first need for men practitioners was therefore met through the appointment of a few men who held administrative or sub-administrative positions and who desired some part-time direct practice. ALCS offered such persons the opportunity for direct practice experience without violating their concept of themselves as self-directing persons, which indeed they were. Qualifications of those selected were the same as for the regular staff, except that it was anticipated that their competence in direct practice might not be equal to that of the regular staff, who had had more sustained, concentrated treatment experience. They did, however, meet the other criteria, particularly that of being self-directing persons. Their responsibility included a group meeting which preceded their evening of work. This was for consultation to each other, to define and follow any program of learning they desired and sought as essential for themselves. Eventually additional part-time staff were added for the purpose of increasing the quantity of service available for clients. All additions to the evening group involved the participation of those present in the selection of the new staff member.

The evening group members were extremely interested in the pilot program and in the structure that evolved. Their comments were sought periodically. Two of the evening group introduced some structural changes in their own agencies, based on the idea that eventually staff should be fully responsible for their own practice. Their experience provided ALCS with some sidelights on the problems of integrating a full-cost service into a philanthropic agency and also of selecting staff able to carry full responsibility for the quality of service they offered in an agency in which experience and competence covered a wide range. (See also footnote 107.)

12.   Because of the author's active participation in the various NASW committees (1959 on) dealing with components of competence, method of assessment, etc., she finds it hard to recall what her own original ideas were. In writing this section she has relied upon notes kept on interviews with candidates, minutes of discussions with staff and at board meetings, and the recollection of a few colleagues, not on ALCS staff, of their own application interviews with her early in the history of ALCS.

13.   In 1954 there was still considerable ferment within the profession concerning the so-called functional vs. diagnostic approach. Though the current state of this controversy is not entirely clear, it is to be noted that some of the concepts of the functional school are now incorporated into the diagnostic and/or crisis theories.

14.   Perhaps because ALCS was known as a pilot program, most agencies concurred with the request to review a candidate's records. They assumed that ALCS would maintain the same professional

responsibility toward their clients as toward its own. In only one instance did the question of confidentiality arise. This agency was willing to have the candidate's practice examined if the candidate would go to the trouble of disguising the record. In most instances, the records were sent to ALCS by registered mail or special messenger. In a few instances, the agency requested that the author read the records in its office.

15.   Candidates who reached this point were usually competent practitioners. In one instance, in inviting a candidate to join staff, the Executive Director suggested that he might want to give thought to the validity of an inference in his references that he took advantage of sick leave. It was made clear that this was not a question here but one that he must face for himself. If chronic illness created the need for frequent absences, this would not only affect the over-all financial responsibility of staff, but would also affect what he could expect to earn. It the inference were valid, then he would also need to consider his ability to discipline himself in view of the different responsibility undertaken for the financial solvency of this agency. An example of a discussion with a rejected candidate is the following: In reading his cases, all of staff noted occasional serious failure to understand a client's message—a "blind spot" in what he did or did not see. This was discussed with him as a staff question about his being invited to join, unless in further discussion it was felt that he was not being assessed correctly. His response indicated a correct evaluation, that he was in treatment, and that this was a general problem in his relationships. He saw this as coming under control, however. He accepted the suggestion that he reapply at a later date if he were still interested in joining ALCS staff.

16.   When drug therapy became available for the treatment of emotionally disturbed persons, a policy decision had to be made. How could one provide such service to those ALCS clients who might benefit from it? The question was introduced by the consultant in psychiatry at a staff meeting and was pursued with members of the Technical Advisory Committee. The policy agreed upon was that the client would be encouraged to discuss with his physician whether it was advisable for him to have such therapy. If he had no personal physician, he could avail himself of ALCS consultants in psychiatry and internal medicine. They then could advise him and, if they desired, they took on the responsibility for adjusting dosage and for periodic review of the effect of drug therapy as well as continued need for it. If they preferred not to go beyond consultation, no drug

would be provided and the client would be given a list of qualified physicians from whom to select one. The consultant would then be available to the physician, if desired. The board was informed of the policy established.

17.   Among those consulted were Dr. Marianne Kris and Dr. Berta Borenstein, both of whom provided a list of highly competent child analysts.

18.   Such consultations might be from psychiatry, medicine, or psychology, but also were at times from other social workers, sociologists, anthropologists, nutritionists, etc.

19.   As noted earlier, the Executive Director took all calls for initial appointments.

20.   In the last two years the hiring and supervision of clerical personnel was shared as described by the office manager, Mrs. Barbara Frank, and Garrath A. Germain, who was hired as a half-time administrative assistant and half-time practitioner.

21.   This was an error on the part of the Executive Director who had too many roles: presenting data for the agenda, answering questions posed by the committee, and summing up decisions. Role confusion did occur, making it appear at times that she was not consulting but defending a point of view. When the error was apparent, she suggested that the committee appoint a chairman from among themselves, but they did not do so. They saw the problems experienced as minor because of the mutuality of professional objectives. However, in the discussions leading to the Technical Advisory Committee report in 1963, the Executive Director asked Mrs. Cathryn S. Guyler to serve as chairman of the meeting. The latter formulated the initial premises for discussion, rewrote the draft for the Technical Advisory Committee's review and approval, and wrote the final report.

22.   Family agencies, or those who meet the criteria for membership in the Family Service Association of America, offer a variety of services often referred to as "concrete." These services are the provision of homemaker service, service to the aged and to the foreign-born, and so forth. ALCS would not have qualified for membership in FSAA because it offered only one service, that of counseling. The FSAA had asked, however, that the agency apply for membership because it was interested in testing out its potential future relationship to similar extensions of service to the economically advantaged, both in relation to program needed and to the method of determining dues paid to FSAA by nonphilanthropic agencies. Had ALCS

continued, it would probably have done so.

23.    Besides services of this nature rendered through psychiatrists and psychologists, there was a similar movement in pastoral counseling (to extend beyond religious questions), in school guidance programs manned by teachers, and among other professions such as medicine and the law. The array of professional groups offering counseling was often confusing to the client seeking help and still continues as a problem. The public cannot always distinguish which profession might be most suited to meet the need for help.

24.    For a fuller discussion, see Chapter 4, *2. Staff Relations.*

25.    Ruth Shallitt and Evelyn Hyman. Eventually they discontinued some of these services and their agency is now known as the Counseling Employment Service.

26.    Among those consulted on fees and other aspects of designing the service were Dr. J. Lester Gabrilove, Dr. M. Ralph Kaufman, Dr. Milton Levine, Dr. Ralph E. Moloshok, Dr. Norman Pleshette, Dr. Iago Galdston, Dr. Arthur F. Anderson, Wilson Parkhill, Mrs. Virginia Wagner, Mrs. Millicent MacIntosh, and Dr. Mitchell Gratwick.

27.    See *7. Production* under *Conditions of Employment and Personnel Practices* later in this chapter.

28.    Only one agency reported (1954) that its fee scale went as high as $25.00 per interview. However, the average fee for that agency was reported between $3.00 and $4.00. All other agencies had weekly fees (regardless of the number of interviews held) and these did not exceed $10.00. In one instance the agency was limited by charter to a fee of $3.00. In 1954, the author also inquired of mental health associations what they considered was the usual fee for psychiatric help. They said that the minimum fee of a psychiatrist was $15.00.

29.    The length of the interview was arbitrarily established and clients were informed of it. It was set originally to permit scheduling of appointments on an hourly basis, allowing 15 minutes for note-taking and preparation for the next interview.

30.    The term *practice* rather than *caseload* is used in this report to emphasize the ALCS philosophy of responsibilities toward clients. *Caseload* seemed to reflect an employee relationship to the agency, the client being the client of the *agency.* Thus when the employee leaves the agency, his caseload remains with it. *Practice* is used because of the connotation that the *practitioner* has a direct responsibility to the client, which does not terminate at the point when the practitioner wants to leave the agency. This term was also preferred

because, early in the development of the pilot project, all began to envision a different relationship between agency and staff. This was a relationship that meant that a person could work within an agency setting, developing his practice, with the expectation of conditions favoring his continuance with the agency on an indefinite basis.

To build a practice consistent with the expectation of 5.4 interviews per day, it was found that staff members would have to schedule between 27 and 30 interviews per week. This would allow for some flucturation due to cancellations.

31.   See earlier section, *The Administrative Structure.*

32.   This hypothesis needs to be validated.

33.   A study of the differences between dictating for an agency folder record and keeping longhand notes might be valuable. See Chapter 4, *Structure and the Issue of Accountability.*

34.   See later sections 7. *Production,* and 12. *Salaries,* on pages 79 and 84, respectively.

35.   Social agencies, to all of which ALCS could have referred with confidence, had large waiting lists of their own. In fact, when their clients could afford the fees, these agencies referred them to ALCS.

36.   The private practitioners who agreed to participate in these discussions were Clara Rabinowitz, Emily Ann Black, Mrs. Mina Holtzberg, Martin Kasten, Louise Connor, Edith Beck, Dorothy Duneaff, Paul Woolf, Mrs. Bernice Gordon, Mrs. Mildred Bergum, and Mrs. Celia Mitchell. Board members who participated were Mrs. Benjamin J. Buttenwieser and Mrs. Garret J. Garretson II. The participation of two persons from NASW (Joseph P. Anderson and Bertram Beck) helped coordinate ALCS efforts with previous work done by that organization concerning social workers in private practice. Their participation in the committee may have been a factor in the subsequent request of the NASW Commission on Practice that the New York City Chapter establish a committee to study the question of whether private practice was possible in social work. The New York City Chapter asked Mrs. Cathryn S. Guyler, serving on a special project for ALCS, and the author to act as co-chairmen. The committee's work coincided with a similar assignment to the Southern Minnesota NASW Chapter to look into the question of licensing or legal regulation for the profession. The New York City Chapter saw the private practice of social work as in keeping with the definition of social work and recommended that standards be set for such practice. The Southern Minnesota Chapter proposed

that NASW engage in some self-regulation preliminary to eventual legal regulation, for which they believed the profession was not quite ready.

In 1958, the NASW Delegate Assembly approved a program of voluntary certification. One of the points stressed was the need for setting standards. In 1960, the Academy of Certified Social Workers was established, with the charge to its board of directors to set qualitative standards of competence for membership. Following this the NASW Commission on Competence set up a study committee under the leadership of Mrs. Ruth Knee, which was eventually charged with establishing standards for independent practice, whether under agency auspices or privately. The work of this committee was completed when guidelines for the assessment of competence had been established and issued. A new committee under Dr. Louis Carr was then established with the charge of determining the feasibility of assessing competence and, if warranted, establishing a method of doing so. Its work culminated in 1971 with the establishment of the Certification for Competence Board. The experience of ALCS was available to all these committees. With the ALCS board's concurrence the author accepted the invitation to be an active member of each of these committees, as part of ALCS's obligation to the profession resulting from its pilot venture.

37.    For a description of this program, see Ruth Fizdale, "Formalizing the Relationship Between Private Practitioners and Social Agencies," *Social Casework* (December 1959).

38.    At one point the Technical Advisory Committee suggested that the agency expand the group of its affiliates to include persons who met ALCS criteria for staff membership but who had not worked in ALCS. This action was never taken because of the inability to offer experience other than direct counseling of clients. The affiliate role could only be attractive to the private practitioner if it provided an opportunity to use his experience in an activity other than direct counseling, such as supervision, teaching, or participation in research, which ALCS could not offer. Contrary to the expectations of some, the private practitioner was less interested in the referrals he might secure as an affiliate than in the opportunity of making available to social agencies (as well as testing out) what he believed the experience of private practice contributed to his competence.

39.    See Appendix 2 for copy of *Fact Sheet*.

40.    Medical social workers, caseworkers and administrators in adoption work, and faculties of schools of social work were among

those invited. The purpose was both to secure their counsel and to keep them informed of the goal and its potential values to them and to social work. The ALCS internist invited a number of physicians for an evening meeting. The consultant in psychiatry invited psychiatrists and a few physicians who had made referrals to him.

41. Victor Weingarten Associates served as consultants.

42. *Our First Two Years* (New York: Arthur Lehman Counseling Service, 1958).

43. (For purposes of clarity, personnel practices for professional staff are described in the body of the report, those for clerical staff are footnoted.) Clerical staff vacations started at three weeks per year and were increased in two years to five weeks. Salaries for clerical staff were consistent with prevailing wages for similar personnel in social agencies.

44. See later sections *7. Production* and *12. Salaries* in this chapter.

45. The change did not affect clerical staff, who still received five days for religious holiday observance. Evening and part-time staff were never covered by policies on vacations, sick leave, religious holidays or personal leave. Also see note 63.

46. The same policy applied to clerical staff.

47. Sick leave taken by professional and clerical staff was so minimal that it was not considered necessary to set a different sick leave policy for the clerical staff. In 1967, a receptionist asked for what seemed an excessive amount of time to undergo elective surgery. Policy for clerical staff was then established in relation to illness requiring a prolonged absence from the agency. The amount of time covered by sick leave would depend upon the diagnosis, length of normal treatment, and anticipated complications. The clerical staff member's physician's recommendations would be discussed with the consultant in medicine and their decision would form the base for allowable paid sick leave. See *Other Findings* in the final section of Chapter 4.

48. See *6. Insurances* which follows.

49. See *12. Salaries* later in this chapter.

50. The master schedule of appointments at the receptionist's desk gave required data regarding the number of interviews held and the fees paid or to be billed. Similarly, bills showed time spent with consultants.

51. This level of production was often possible for a practitioner who had worked in the agency six months and was certain for those

who had been with ALCS for a full year.

52. The policy also applied to evening and part-time practitioners. Clerical staff were hired with a probationary period of three months.

53. See earlier section, *Administrative Structure.* This policy applied to both evening and part-time staff. No formal period of evaluation was held with clerical staff. Problems were discussed as needs arose. Increments were given if clerical staff were retained. The intimate atmosphere of a small staff makes it easy to deal with evaluations informally. Clerical staff were well aware of how they were regarded by all of professional staff. The relationship was informal and obviously great respect existed among clerical staff for professional staff, despite occasional annoyances.

54. The policy on resignation in most social agencies is based on the concept that the client is and sees himself as the client of the agency. A month's notice had been found a reasonable period of time to inform the client of the practitioner's leaving and theoretically to help him react to the sense of loss and to accept transfer to another practitioner. In this period, the practitioner can also complete all administrative tasks of a caseload—dictation, collection of fees, etc.; it also allows a reasonable length of time for finding a replacement.

55. See earlier section, *Affiliate Program and the Waiting List,* in this chapter.

56. The Executive Director had not seen herself as an employee but rather as a professional person joining with the board in the exploration of a pilot program. She had worked on the basis of an implicit understanding that, in any pilot venture of a professional nature, the professional makes the decisions, using the board in an advisory capacity. The board's action meant a reversal of that understanding regarding the board-executive relationship.

57. See *Costs, Source of Income and Accountability,* Chapter 4.

58. At first board and staff expressed some concern over the recommendation. Staff's initial concern was that this method would require their giving up another evening to earn more from "extra" interviews. Obviously this was a transfer of experience from another agency and not consistent with their experience at ALCS. (See earlier section, *8. Work Week.*) A review of their actual production showed that they were doing more than five interviews a day, that they were held responsible for production and for participation in the pilot venture, which required their being in for appointments and

meetings and that their schedules were already responsive to client needs. Staff were then able to see that taking extra interviews did not imply giving up extra evenings. Some of the board expressed concern over this suggestion, because there was to be no set limit upon the number of extra interviews a staff member could carry. This was a momentary concern and yielded to the recognition that no system of salary in itself guaranteed quality of service. In the final analysis, quality of service is always dependent upon the professional integrity of the practitioner.

59. The rationale for this action appears in the minutes of the Administrative Committee of June 1961: "Since the board carries financial responsibility for ALCS, it shall determine how a contingency fund should be built and what percentage of each year's income should be allocated for the building of such reserves and what percentage may be distributed to staff. Staff, as long as they are in an employee status, will not participate in these decisions but recommendations will be sought from them concerning how bonuses will be given, that is, do they prefer these as cash grants, in the form of fringe benefits, and if so, what kind...? Final decision regarding the adoption, modification or rejection of such recommendations will rest with the board in accordance with what is administratively most feasible and in keeping with the overall purpose of self-support."

60. The board viewed costs of insurance, clerical assistance, seminars, office maintenance, etc., as included in salary comparisons with those in private practice who must meet such costs out of their income.

61. Only the Finance Committee included all regular staff. All other committees had an equal number of staff and board. Since all regular staff were involved in financing the agency, it was essential that all fully understand budgeting and alternative choices in meeting costs of agency operation. To have excluded some would be to invite problems of "representation" and negotiation.

62. The client may not always be accurate in his appraisal of the quality of a professional service he is receiving. However, he does pay willingly whatever he sees as a fair rate for his estimate of the quality of service he receives.

63. Evening and part-time staff received a fee for every interview held or charged for. Initially they were paid $30.00 an evening with the expectation that three interviews would be held or charged for, as in cancellations. However, evening staff became uncomfortable when a new client could not be immediately assigned after another

had terminated treatment. They preferred to be paid by the interview. They then received $10.00 for each interview; later this was increased to $12.50 and finally to $15.00. This was the same compensation as regular staff received for "extra" interviews.

The policy followed in giving increments for the executive was that she receive the same increments as staff when these were made possible by fee increases. However, the amount received was in proportion to the time spent in administering the service program. When in 1969 base salaries were changed because of the higher number of interviews actually sustained by all, no increase was made in the Executive Director's salary.

64.   This staff member did gradually reduce his work week in the agency to two and one-half days. However, he attended all staff meetings, even when these occurred on days that he was not scheduled to be in the agency. He also carried out all responsibilities in the conduct of the program administratively without any question.

65.   See earlier section, *11. Resignations.*

66.   See *Report of the Ad Hoc Committee on Private Practice,* November 30, 1966, in Appendix 4.

67.   Minutes of the Board of Directors meeting, March, 1967, include the open concern of some members with this decision. It raised for them again the question of their proper role. However, consensus was in favor of an advisory role to staff, in this instance.

68.   This impression is based upon the author's having invited six research persons to review the goals of ALCS. They made brief studies of ALCS practice and experience to identify what would be possible to research, to further both the goals of the pilot program and the knowledge of the profession. All six offered extremely interesting proposals but all of these were related in some form to the major area of their own research interest and not specifically to the ALCS aims.

69.   The Technical Advisory Committee suggested that a report be made on most of these points.

70.   Up to this point there had always been on staff either a part-time consultant in public relations or a person carrying out a defined public relations task.

71.   Included in this category were lawyers, dentists, teachers, physicians, nurses, actors, psychologists and social workers.

72.   Included in this group were executives in public relations firms, in large-scale industries, representatives to the United Nations, stockbrokers, governmental officials and small shopkeepers.

73.    A proportion of ALCS clients, varying from 10% to almost 33% in some years, did not wish to disclose their income, or the practitioner failed to record the information, or no logical occasion for inquiry arose. Generally, information would be given as the client was discussing some question he had in which income was relevant to the point he was making.

74.    See Appendix 3, Table XI of *Report from Blanche Bernstein to Ruth Fizdale.*

75.    Blanche Bernstein, "Income Distribution in New York City," *The Public Interest* (July 1970).

76.    See Appendix 3, *Report from Blanche Bernstein to Ruth Fizdale.*

77.    Included· in the group of social agencies that referred clients to ALCS are not only the family agencies of New York City and suburban towns, but also such agencies as offer referral and information services—community councils and mental health associations. Child guidance, adoption and mental health agencies also referred, as well as social service departments of hospitals. A few referrals were also received from social agencies of cities across the United States.

78.    See Appendix 3, *Report from Blanche Bernstein to Ruth Fizdale.*

79.    The FSAA categorizes cases according to number of interviews held. To make our figures comparable, we used the same definitions: BSA means that the client never went beyond calling or requesting an appointment. BSB indicates there was at least one in-person interview. CSA means there were two to five interviews. CSB means there were six or more.

80.    See Appendix 3, *Report from Blanche Bernstein to Ruth Fizdale.*

81.    Martin Greenberg, "Practitioner Judgments on Cases Closed, July 1965, to June 1967." (unpublished paper).

82.    See Chapter 2, *Type of Service,* and note 25.

83.    See Appendix 5, *Report of Technical Advisory Committee to Board of Directors,* October, 1963.

84.    See Appendix 3, *Report from Blanche Bernstein to Ruth Fizdale.*

85.    Blanche Bernstein, ibid., note 75.

86.    Ibid.

87.    Flll-cost fees will vary from community to community since salaries for practitioners and clerical personnel, rentals for

offices, and so on, do vary. Therefore, fees set by ALCS cannot be viewed as necessarily covering full cost in other communities.

88.   The Stamford Family and Children's Services, the Family Service Association of Palo Alto, and the Westchester Jewish Community Services. Excluded from the report is the fee-charging for social services established in 1958 at Beth Israel Hospital in Boston, Massachusetts, because no direct advance consultation was held with ALCS.

89.   The Stamford Family and Children's Services opened the Mary Richmond Clinic, and the Westchester Jewish Community Services opened the Clarence Whitehill Counseling Service.

90.   Similar questions were raised by the Federation of Jewish Philanthropies of New York City when the Clarence Whitehill Counseling Service was set up. Apparently experience did not show the concern to be valid.

See Leonard Rohmer, "A Self-Maintaining, Fee-Supported Division of a Family Agency: The Clarence Whitehill Counseling Service," presented at the annual meeting of the National Conference on Jewish Communal Service, Philadelphia, Pa., June 1, 1965.

91.   See Administrative Structure, introductory section.

92.   See Administrative Structure, *a. Criteria for Staff Selection.*

93.   See note 6.

94.   Ruth Fizdale, "Peer Group Supervision," *Social Casework* (October 1958).

95.   Social workers viewed with alarm, for example, the growing trend in psychiatry toward family-oriented treatment; psychiatrists were equally concerned with the growing counseling and psychotherapeutic services of social workers and psychologists.

96.   The content and leaders of some of the seminars held in the agency follow:

*Conjoint Treatment of Marital Discord*, Dr. Bela Mittelmann.
*Treatment of Schizophrenics, Diagnosis and Problems*, Dr. Gustav Bychowski.
*The Development of Psychoanalytic Theory and Its Use in Psychotherapy*, Martin S. Bergmann.
*Manifest Content of Dreams, Their Use in Psychotherapy*, Martin S. Bergmann.
*The Male Homosexual, Diagnostic and Treatment Problems*, Martin S. Bergmann.
*The Female Homosexual, Diagnostic and Treatment Problems*, Martin S. Bergmann.

*The Schizophrenic, Diagnostic and Treatment Problems,*
Martin S. Bergmann.
*The Borderline Personality, Diagnostic and Treatment Problems,* Martin S. Bergmann.
*The Contributions of Social Work to Psychotherapy,*
Martin S. Bergmann.
*Problems of Termination,* Martin S. Bergmann.
*Complex Factors in Ego Development and their Effect and Implications for the Treatment Process,* Martin S. Bergmann.
*The Development of the Ego,* Mrs. Maria Bergmann.
*Group Counseling,* Sanford N. Sherman.

In addition, brief (one to five sessions) consultations were held with a number of other persons. Among those consulted in group meetings were Dr. Jules V. Coleman, Dr. Otto Pollak, Mrs. Frances Scherz. Mrs. Helen Harris Perlman as a guest was a catalyst in a discussion on agency role with adolescents on questions of sexuality.

97. Dr. Nathan S. Ackerman.

98. Among those consulted before deciding whether ALCS would offer group therapy were Mrs. Asya Kadis, Dr. Alexander Wolf, Dr. Hannah Grunewald, Sanford N. Sherman. Mr. Sherman was asked to serve as a leader for a seminar dealing with the initiation and conduct of a group therapy program. This seminar ended when the first group was formed. Later the practitioner carrying a group in therapy secured consultation from Dr. Helen Durkin on a continuous basis for a year.

99. See note 98.

100. Rigmor Erickson (Asmundsson), "Counseling After Legal Adoption in a Family Centered Agency," presented at a Child Welfare League of America meeting, 1961 (unpublished).

Ruth A. Baker, "Principles of Marriage Counseling," presented at New Jersey State Welfare Conference, October 1963 (unpublished).

Freda F. Moss, "Parental Concerns about Adolescents: Their Implications for Family Mental Health," *Child Study Association of America Journal* (out of print).

Alice Fine, "Purpose and Structure of Marital Counseling," presented at Missouri-Kansas NASW Institute, 1965 (unpublished).

Rubin Blanck, "Marriage as a Phase of Personality Development," presented at Missouri-Kansas NASW Institute, *Social Casework* (March 1965).

Rubin Blanck, "The Development of a Professional Self," presented at National Conference on Social Welfare, Los Angeles, California, May 1964 (unpublished).

Rubin Blanck, "The Case for Individual Treatment," *Social Casework* (February 1965).

Toby Kramerson (Jacobson), "Treatment of Borderline Personalities," presented at the American Orthopsychiatric Association conference, San Francisco, California, 1966 (unpublished).

In 1965, the Missouri-Kansas NASW Chapter invited ALCS to lead a seminar for them in the spring of that year. In preparation for this, ALCS held a series of staff meetings trying to isolate ideas that might be presented at such a seminar. Subsequently individual staff members took responsibility for writing papers dealing with specific points disucssed. The papers by Alice Fine and Rubin Blanck were used as the basis of the seminar conducted in Kansas City. The author assumed responsibility for its leadership. Mr. Blanck's paper was the beginning of his idea for a book written in collaboration with his wife, Dr. Gertrude Blanck, *Marriage and Personal Development* (New York: Columbia University Press, 1968).

The paper by Toby Kramerson, cited above, was prepared also for possible use in the Missouri-Kansas NASW seminar. However, it was reserved for presentation at the American Orthopsychiatric Association conference in San Francisco. A fourth paper prepared for the seminar was written by Freda Moss and Milan Stoeger, examining the potential relationship between the personality problems of marital pairs and the point in their marriage at which counseling was sought. Were there observable differences in the personalities of the pairs who sought marital counseling within the first year of marriage, for example, from those who sought help when children left home? This paper was never completed since the two authors felt that they needed to do additional study before presentation.

101.   Dr. David Fanshel began his social work career as a practitioner and later entered research. To revive for himself the "feel" of practice, he requested permission to carry one or two cases under supervision. This was arranged. He also participated equally as a member of the evening group. In addition, he attended the regular staff group meetings when he could. His serious involvement won

him the respect and confidence of the staff. While other research persons may not seek a similar return to practice experience, their understanding of the process of treatment is essential for staff respect.

102. The project submitted to and approved by the National Institute of Mental Health was a study of "The Cognitive Aspects of Treatment Decisions of Experienced Casework Practitioners." It involved the taping of interviews held with families over a span of time (to which they had consented). These were reviewed in sessions where the researcher and the practitioner listened to the taped interviews, stopping at points to discuss specific questions set for the project. The exchanges between the research persons (Dr. David Fanshel and/or Dr. Herbert Aptekar) and the practitioner were recorded as they occurred at the points of the play-back of the treatment session. These second tapes were then analyzed. One of the products of this research is a teaching package written by Dr. David Fanshel and Mrs. Freda F. Moss, *Play-Back: A Marriage in Jeopardy Reviewed* (New York: Columbia University Press, 1972).

A second volume, in preparation by Dr. Fanshel and Dr. William Labov of the University of Pennsylvania, will deal with a method of analyzing the paralingual manifestations in interviews as these relate to treatment. (No title for this book has as yet been agreed upon). It is expected that other volumes will be published, one of which will be an analysis of the material in relation to the initial goals of the research grant, namely, the cognitive aspects of treatment decisions. This research was made possible first by the "seed" money grant of the Adele and Arthur Lehman Foundation, by funding from the National Institute of Mental Health, and a subsequent additional grant from the John L. Loeb Foundation, covering some of the unexpected costs of the expanded goals of the initial research project. Costs of publication were underwritten by the Adele and Arthur Lehman Foundation.

An important aspect of the NIMH grant was the approval of payment to the agency for time used by staff members in play-back sessions (in reviewing interviews with the research person). Payment was made on the same basis as fees charged clients for 45-minute interviews. The practitioner was then credited for this time, as for interviews completed, in the computing of additional compensation for extra interviews.

103. See section 7. *Production,* Chapter 2.

104. As a supervisor at the Jewish Family Service of Brooklyn

in the 1940's, the author was encouraged by the Executive Director, Mrs. Gertrude R. Davis, to test her hypotheses about sound termination of supervision. Later, when the author was the Assistant Executive Director, she was responsible for selection of practitioner staff. Here she based her work partly upon the methods used by Mrs. Davis in selection of staff, and was encouraged to test out staff selection as requiring the application of casework knowledge to a different but essential social agency process.

105. See Section, *Case Records and Recording,* Chapter 1.

106. See section, *1. The Board of Directors,* Chapter 1.

107. Excluded from this report is a second group that was formed to evaluate the usefulness of preparing selected practitioners for regular employment at ALCS. These were people who were experienced but not in direct practice. In addition, one casework faculty member of a school of social work agreed to join this group to see whether a direct practice opportunity would indeed enrich her teaching. The group did receive group supervision in preparation for full accountability. It was disbanded in less than two years because of several factors that made experimentation difficult. The failure of the experiment was in part occasioned by administrative problems outside the control of the group.

108. Irving Greenberg, Executive Director of Jewish Counseling and Service Agency of Essex County, Newark, N.J., and William Gioseffi, Chief Social Worker, Veterans Administration Regional Office, New York City.

109. This loan was repaid by the Park East Counseling Group in keeping with the initial contractual agreement, which included payment of interest and return of capital.

110. See sections, *Type of Service,* Chapter 1; *11. Resignations,* Chapter 2; and *Costs, Source of Income and Accountability,* Chapter 4.

111. See *Guidelines for the Assessment of Professional Practice in Social Work* (New York National Association of Social Workers, 1968), Ruth I. Knee, Chairman, Committee on Study of Competence.

112. The term *psychological factors* includes those that are inherent in the giving and taking of philanthropic assistance, or help in any form, as well as those brought by the individual client as part of his personality and way of functioning.

113. See Chapter 2.

114. This would change some of the processes of hiring staff and inviting board, with greater emphasis upon their opportunity to

examine their interest in the program itself. See Chapter 1, *3b. The Hiring Process.*

115.   S. P. Goldberg, "Accounting in Social Welfare," *Encyclopedia of Social Work,* Robert Morris, ed. Vol. I, pp. 2-8 (New York: National Association of Social Workers, 1971).

# Appendix I

## Members of the ALCS Board of Directors

Mrs. Arthur Lehman** ..................................................... Founder
Chairman of the Board, 1954-65
Mrs. Richard J. Bernhard** ............................................... Founder
President of the Board, 1954-64
Vice-President ........... 1964-68
Mrs. Benjamin J. Buttenwieser ........................................... Founder
Vice-President ........... 1954-61
Mrs. John L. Loeb ........................................................... Founder
Vice-President ........... 1954-
Ira M. Younker*** .......................................................... Founder
Treasurer ................... 1954-57
Dr. Maurice B. Hexter ..................................................... Founder

Robert A. Bernhard* ...................... Associate Treasurer ... 1954-59
Lawrence B. Buttenwieser ............................. Treasurer ... 1964-
Mrs. Harold D. Harvey ..................................... Secretary ... 1954-64
President ... 1964-
Mrs. Arthur F. Anderson ................................. Secretary ... 1964-

William L. Bernhard ....................... Member-at-Large ....... 1967-
Dr. Leonard W. Mayo* ................... Member-at-Large ....... 1966-67
Mrs. Sophia M. Robison** ............. Member-at-Large ....... 1954-69
Mrs. Garret J. Garretson II* .......... Member-at-Large ....... 1956-66

*Continued on next page*

Stirling S. Adams                              *Dr. Marion E. Kenworthy
John Burke**                                    *Katharine F. Lenroot
Mrs. Marco Chiara***                          **Mrs. Michael Loeb
Mrs. Edwin F. Chinlund                        **Msgr. James J. Lynch
Dr. Jules V. Coleman                        ***Bishop Francis J. Mugavero
Loula F. Dunn*                                   Robert H. Mulreany
Marshall Field**                                    Wilson Parkhill
Henry J. Friendly*                              George N. Shuster
Mrs. C. Gerald Goldsmith***            Mrs. Clarence Whitehill

*Members, Honorary Board.      **Deceased.      ***Resigned.

Others who offered individual consultation and other assistance

Bertram Beck                                  Helen Harris Perlman
Sidney J. Berkowitz                                   Joseph Reid
Eleanor Cranefield                                 Frances Scherz
Melvin Glasser                                           Jerry Solon
Arthur Kruse                                     Dr. Herman Stein

Frederika Neumann

Technical Advisory Committee Members

*Community Service Society*                   Dr. Stanley P. Davies
                                                  George Hallwachs
                                                      Frank Hertel
                                               Mrs. Mildred Kilinski

*Jewish Family Service*                    Mrs. Frances L. Beatman
                                             Dr. Robert M. Gomberg
                                                Sanford N. Sherman

*Brooklyn Bureau of Social*                   Frederick I. Daniels
*Services*                                          Frank Greving
                                                 Margaret Kaufman

*Catholic Charities of the*                   Rev. Robert A. Ford
*Archdiocese of New York*                     Rosemary Sheridan

*Family Service Association*
*of America*                                   Clark W. Blackburn

*National Association of*
*Social Workers*                              Joseph P. Anderson

## Professional Staff Members

| | Years on | | Next Professional Role |
| --- | --- | --- | --- |
| | Regular Staff | Part-time Staff | |
| Mrs. Blanche (Zebine) Lyons | 4 + 4 mos. | 7 yrs. | Private practice. |
| Mrs. Sylvia (Rubin) Dilman | 2 | | Caseworker-senior in west coast agency. |
| Rebecca Eikenberry | 2 | | Casework consultant in midwest agency. |
| Catherine Donnell | 3 | 3 | Casework supervisor in New York agency. |
| Alice Fine | 13 + 9 mos. | | Park East Counseling Group. |
| Mrs. Ruth A. Baker | 10 | | Private practice. |
| Rubin Blanck | 10 + 6 mos. | | Private practice. |
| Monica Haller | 4 | 1 | Administrator in New York agency. |
| Mrs. Freda F. Moss | 10 + 4 mos. | | Park East Counseling Group. |
| Mrs. Rigmor Asmundsson | 3 | 6 | Casework supervisor in Conn. agency. |
| Mrs. Toby Kramerson | 8 | | Private practice. |
| Milan Stoeger | 9 + 10 mos. | | Park East Counseling Group. |
| Ruth Cuker | 2 | | Private practice. |
| Mrs. Florence A. Gadol | 5 + 3 mos. | | Park East Counseling Group. |
| Margrit Wreschner | 3 + 2 mos. | | Park East Counseling Group. |
| Garrath A. Germain | 2 + 3 mos. | | Park East Counseling Group. |
| Irene Harmos | 1 + 6 mos. | 6 mos. | Casework supervisor in New York agency; part-time Park East Counseling Group. |
| Marlene Menifee | 9 mos. | | Park East Counseling Group. |

## Part-Time Staff

| Group I | Group II | Group III |
|---|---|---|
| George Frank | Mrs. Trudy Feintuch | Edith Beck |
| William Gioseffi | Theodore Hackman | Marvin Scherer |
| Irving Greenberg | Maria Modica | Rena Schulman |
| Mrs. Rae Retzker | Dr. William Reid | |
| Sylvia Solovey | Isabel Stamm | |
| | Mrs. Winifred Vetter | |

## Research Staff

Dr. Herbert H. Aptekar
Dr. David Fanshel
Dr. William Labov

## Consultants

*Fiscal Management & Statistics:* Blanche Bernstein
Martin Greenberg
Florence Zunser

*Legal:* Mrs. Benjamin J. Buttenwieser
Samuel Fagelman

*Psychiatry:* Martin S. Bergmann
Dr. Sol W. Ginsburg
Dr. Edward J. Hornick

*Medicine:* Dr. Gary Zucker

*Psychology:* Dr. Miriam Siegel

*Public Relations:* Mrs. Cathryn S. Guyler
Mrs. Marion Sanders
Victor Weingarten

## Clerical Staff

### Office Managers

Barbara B. Frank                        Joanne Murie Miller
Lillian Kaplan                            Kay Overholt
Beatrice Trachtenberg Michaels

### Receptionists

Dolores Angleton Guarnieri                    Nina Kimche
Miriam Kaminsky                    Doris Peterson Marshall
Barbara Bagnall Scheffler

# Appendix II

Reproduction of *Fact Sheet*

### ARTHUR LEHMAN COUNSELING SERVICE
1382 Lexington Avenue
New York, N.Y. 10028

This fact-sheet contains basic information about a new venture in personal and family counseling under the auspices of the Adele and Arthur Lehman Foundation. Members of the board and the executive director will be glad to discuss the project with interested individuals or agencies. Particularly welcome are constructive suggestions from associates in the counseling field, physicians, psychiatrists, attorneys, educators and others concerned with problems of human relations.

Mrs. Arthur Lehman, Chairman

Mrs. Richard J. Bernhard, President

Mrs. Arthur Forrest Anderson
Mrs. Richard N. Beaty
Robert A. Bernhard
Mrs. Benjamin J. Buttenwieser
John Burke
Mrs. Edwin F. Chinlund
Dr. Jules V. Coleman
Miss Loula F. Dunn
Marshall Field
Henry J. Friendly
Mrs. Harold D. Harvey

Dr. Marion E. Kenworthy
Miss Katharine F. Lenroot
Mrs. John L. Loeb
Mrs. Michael Loeb
Msgr. James J. Lynch
Leonard W. Mayo, S. Sc. D.
Mrs. Sophia M. Robison, Ph. D.
Maurice B. Hexter, Ph. D.
George N. Shuster, Ph. D.
David Sher
Ira M. Younker

Executive Director: Ruth Fizdale

## FACTS ABOUT
## ARTHUR LEHMAN COUNSELING SERVICE

*1.  Why another agency?*
At present, a substantial segment of the community does not use the
counseling services of family agencies, possibly because of the long
identification of social agencies with philanthropy. Yet income level
does not determine incidence of human problems. ALCS is an
independent, nonsectarian, nonprofit organization, which seeks to
extend public understanding and use of casework counseling.

*2.  What is the purpose of ALCS?*
The goal is to help each individual who seeks its counsel to mobilize
his full resources and those of his environment to deal effectively
with the problems of living. ALCS also has a purpose beyond its
service to clients. It is a pilot project which seeks to determine
whether counseling can help the group which has not yet turned to
family agencies and whether the service can be self-supporting.

*3.  With what kinds of problems does ALCS deal?*
The service assists in solving the kinds of problems that can occur in
any family or in the course of any individual's life, such as marital
conflict, difficulties between children and parents, problems of the
aging or family situations complicated by mental or physical illness.
Skilled help given at the onset of trouble can frequently prevent
serious crises.

*4.  Who provides the counseling service?*
The staff consists of experienced caseworkers who have achieved
recognition in the field of family counseling. All hold graduate degrees
from leading schools of social work. The executive director has had
wide experience in casework, teaching and administration in govern-
ment-sponsored and private counseling services. Consultation between
counselors, executive director and staff psychiatrists assures the
highest caliber of professional service.

*5.  What is the relationship of ALCS to psychiatry?*
The counselor works cooperatively with psychiatrists and psychologists, each bringing to the client's problems his special professional
skills. Those who require psychiatric care are aided in becoming
aware of their need and in seeking treatment. Psychiatrists and

psychologists have referred to ALCS the parents of children and other relatives of persons undergoing psychiatric treatment. The role of the counselor, in such situations, is to aid therapy by developing support and understanding in those close to the patient. ALCS has also been called upon to give help to the husbands, wives and children of persons in mental institutions.

6. *What is the relationship of the Service to the medical profession generally?*
General practitioners, internists, pediatricians and other specialists have referred to ALCS patients and their families when recovery could be speeded by greater insight into or adjustment to related environmental factors. Long term or permanently handicapping illnesses frequently engender personal difficulties. In such situations the psychological attitude of the patient and those close to him can play a significant role in therapy. ALCS maintains close collaboration with the referring doctor in the interest of the patient.

7. *What is the relationship of ALCS to the social work profession?*
The Service is seeking answers to questions in which the entire social work profession is deeply concerned. Advising on technical aspects is a committee which at present includes: Stanley P. Davies and Frank J. Hertel of the Community Service Society; M. Robert Gomberg and Mrs. Frances L. Beatman of Jewish Family Service; Reverend Robert A. Ford of Catholic Charities Family Service; Frederick I. Daniels and Frank Greving of Brooklyn Bureau of Social Services; and Herbert H. Aptekar of Jewish Community Services, Queens-Nassau.

8. *Is a charge made?*
Yes. A flat fee of $10 per interview is charged. Although it hopes to operate on a self-sustaining basis, ALCS is a nonprofit undertaking, made possible through the support of the Adele and Arthur Lehman Foundation.

9. *Where is ALCS located?*
At 1382 Lexington Avenue (near 91st Street). The building is a former private residence.

10. *What are ALCS office hours?*
Interviews may be arranged by appointment from 12:30–8:30

Monday and from 9:00 to 5:00 Tuesday through Friday.

11. *What is the function of the Adele and Arthur Lehman*
    *Foundation?*
ALCS is a pilot project consonant with the Lehman family tradition
of practical and forward-looking service to the community. The
Foundation has underwritten initial expenses, as well as continuing
research and demonstration.

# Appendix III

*Report from Blanche Bernstein to Ruth Fizdale*
*The Agency's Growth—1954-55 to 1968-69*

THE GROWTH and development of the Arthur Lehman Counseling Service can be measured in a number of ways—the number of caseworker interviews, the size of the staff, the salaries they were able to earn, the income and expenditures of the agency, the surplus [1] or deficit it incurred, and the charges it made for the service it provided. The history of ALCS spans a period of 15½% years, from the middle of 1954 to the end of 1969. In order to present a picture of the agency's development without burdening the reader with too many figures, we have selected some significant statistics for the first and last full years of ALCS operation and for two years at five-year intervals in between ("Summary of Operations" table).

The number of caseworker interviewers rose from 1472 in 1954-55 to 10,470 in 1968-69, or by about 600 percent. This reflected the gradual increase in staff from an average of 1.6 full-time caseworkers during the first year's operation, to an average of 6.5 full-time and 5.6 part-time caseworkers in 1968-69. Actually, an even higher level of interviews was reached in the years from 1961-62 to 1967-68, with the peak occurring in 1963-64, when 12,493 interviews were held. During this year, both the full and part-time staff were somewhat larger.

The increase in the total number of interviews did not result solely from the enlargement of the casework sraff. The average number of interviews per caseworker also rose from 915 per year in 1954-55 to about 943 in 1968-69. This was, in the main, due to a shift in the salary payment system which resulted in a more efficient use of staff time so that it became possible for each caseworker to do more interviews per week. To some extent, however, it reflected at times additional hours of work for each caseworker.

## SUMMARY OF OPERATIONS

| | 1954-55 | 1958-59 | 1963-64 | 1968-69 |
|---|---|---|---|---|
| Total applications | 396 | 712 | 588 | 456 |
| Accepted for interview | 344 | 659 | 559 | 431 |
| Total interviews | 1,472 | 7,383½ | 12,493 | 10,470 |
| Number of caseworkers: | | | | |
|   Full-time | 1.6 | 4.9 | 6.8 | 6.5 |
|   Part-time | | 6.4 | 6.75 | 5.6 |
| Average no. of interviews | | | | |
|   per week | 28 | 142 | 240.5 | 201.3 |
|   per caseworker per annum* | 915 | 671 | 925.4 | 943.2 |
| Caseworker salary: (1) | | | | |
|   Current dollars | $ 6,000 | $ 7,500 | $ 10,000 (2) | $ 15,000 |
|   Constant dollars (1968-69) | $ 8,286 | $ 9,540 | $ 11,710 | $ 15,000 |
| Average caseworker earnings: | | | | |
|   Current dollars | $ 6,000 | $ 8,350 | $ 13,772 | $ 17,200 |
|   Constant dollars (1968-69) | $ 8,286 | $ 10,621 | $ 16,127 | $ 17,200 |

| | | | |
|---|---|---|---|
| Total counseling income | $ 12,856 | $ 87,463 | $185,978 | $193,595 |
| Total net costs | $ 37,899 | $ 96,939 | $164,784 | $192,170 |
| Surplus (Deficit) | ($ 25,040) | ($ 9,473) | $ 21,194 | $ 1,425 |
| Amount of fees waived | nil | $ 583 | $ 671 | $ 450 |
| Cost per interview (3) | $ 25.86 | $ 13.12 | $ 13.19 | $ 18.35 |
| Fee per interview: | | | | |
| Current dollars | $ 10.00 | $ 12.50 | $ 15.00 | $ 19.25 |
| Constant dollars | $ 13.70 | $ 15.90 | $ 17.65 | $ 19.25 |

(1) All staff received the same base salary. (Earnings include income from additional interviews.)
(2) Includes an end-of-year adjustment of $2,000.
(3) Net expenditures divided by total interviews.
(4) Represents the weighted average of the fee of $17.50 which prevailed from July 1, 1968 to February 28, 1969, and the fee of $22.50 instituted on March 1, 1969.

*[Miss Bernstein computed this average by including part-time staff as well as regular staff. Hence her figures differ from those quoted in the body of the report as production for regular staff.—R.F.]

ALCS was an experiment in many ways. Among the experimental features were not only the type and volume of clientele the agency would attract but what it could provide in salaries and earnings for its caseworkers. Starting at $6,000 in 1954-55, salaries were raised at various intervals and reached $7,500 in 1958-59, $10,000 (including an end-of-year salary adjustment) [2] in 1963-64, and $14,900 in 1968-69. In terms of constant 1968-69 dollars (i.e., taking account of the rise in prices during this period), the rise was from $8,286 to $15,000, or about 81 percent. Looking at caseworker earnings (i.e., salaries, including end-of-year adjustments, plus extra payments for additional interviews), the rise was even more substantial, going from $8,286 in 1954-55 and $10,621 in 1958-59, to $17,200 in 1968-69, in constant dollars, or an increase of about 107 percent.

These years were, of course, a period of rising real incomes for most people in the country as a whole and in New York City. One must ask, therefore, whether ALCS caseworkers did better or worse or about the same as most earners. A rough comparison can be made for the ten-year period 1958-59 to 1968-69. During these years, ALCS caseworker salaries, in constant dollars, rose by 56 percent and caseworker earnings by 62 percent. Median income of New York City white families during approximately the same period rose by about 20 percent, and in part this was due to an increase in the average number of earners per family. [3] Clearly, the ALCS workers did better. A further comparison can and should be made, however, between ALCS caseworkers and senior caseworkers in the voluntary social agencies of New York. Data available from the Community Council of Greater New York indicate that in general salaries of senior caseworkers in New York City agencies rose from $7,660 in 1958 to $10,866 in 1968, in constant dollars, or by 42 percent. Thus in terms of both salary and earnings, the ALCS caseworkers did substantially better.

What is particularly interesting about the favorable situation of the ALCS caseworkers is that it was achieved at the same time that the agency was shifting from a substantial deficit position to a surplus and without imposing excessive charges on the clients. The fee per interview was indeed raised several times, from $10.00 in 1954-55 to $12.50 in 1958-59, to $15.00 in 1963-64, and to an average of $19.25 in 1968-69. [4] In constant dollars, therefore, the fee per interview rose from $13.70 to $19.25, or by 41 percent in the 15-year period, only slightly more than the 37 percent rise in the consumer price index for the New York City region for all goods and services.

As the staff was enlarged and the number of interviews increased, the agency's income as well as its costs went up, but income went up more. ALCS started with a deficit of just about $25,000 in the first year of its operation. This was reduced to about $9,500 by 1958-59 and was completely eliminated in 1960-61. A very substantial surplus of more than $21,000 was achieved in 1963-64, the peak year in terms of size of staff and number of interviews. The amount of surplus was somewhat diminished in each of the succeeding five years as caseworker salaries were increased substantially more proportionately than were fees. By 1968-69, the last full year of operation, the surplus was down to about $1,400. The fee per interview was increased from $17.50 to $22.50 on March 1, 1969, and caseworker salaries were raised to $20,000 as of July 1, 1969.

Two factors explain the shift from the early deficit position to the surplus which was achieved in each year beginning with 1960-61. Within the first five years, the cost per interview was cut almost in half as staff increased and overhead costs were spread over a far larger number of interviews. Second, the fee per interview was gradually brought into line with the cost and finally somewhat exceeded it, thus producing a surplus from the total agency operation for the contingency fund. In 1954-55, the cost per interview was $25.86 and the fee was $10.00. In 1958-59, the cost was $13.12 and the fee $12.50. By 1963-64, the position was reversed. The cost was $13.19 and the fee $15.00, and this position has been maintained since that time, with the margin sometimes narrower and sometimes wider as costs (mainly higher caseworker salaries) began to catch up with the increased income resulting from each of the fee increases. In connection with the development of the agency's financial situation, it is of some interest to note the very low amount of fees which had to be waived because of the client's inability to meet his bills. Fees waived never exceeded one percent of client income and reached that level in only one year (1966). It has dropped as low as one-tenth of one percent and an average has been just about four-tenths of one percent.

## Characteristics of Cases and Clients

A series of tables in this appendix present a variety of data on ALCS cases and clients since the early years of the agency operation.

These data are based on cases closed during the year which had at least one interview. Some of the highlights are given here for the period 1958-59 to 1968-69 when the agency was in full swing.

## 1. Length of Service

Of all the persons who telephoned ALCS to make some inquiry with respect to their problems, from 41 to 53 percent, but generally somewhat less than 50 percent, are closed after the telephone inquiry. This appears to be a very high percentage but it is in line with the experience of most casework agencies. There are a number of reasons for this high drop-out rate: Many are not really ready for counseling; some really want a psychiatrist; some wanted an arbitrator of their marital problems; some were in treatment and, though not satisfied with it, were not ready to change; some were misinformed about the agency's fee policy; and finally, some thought it was an investment counseling agency.

Generally, from 10 to 17 percent have two to five interviews and about 23 to 33 percent have six or more interviews.

There do not seem to be any marked trends in the relative significance of the long- and short-term cases during the last ten years. The variations from year to year appear to be random. Roughly, the average pattern is about 45 percent closed after the telephone inquiry, 13 percent closed after one interview, 14 percent closed after two to five interviews, and 28 percent closed after six or more interviews. Among those who had two to five interviews, the median during the last ten years has been closer to two than to five and has ranged from 3.3 to 2.1 and generally has been 2.4 to 2.5 interviews. Among the long-term cases, those with six or more interviews, the median has ranged from 16 to 29 interviews. The average for the decade has been a median of 23 long-term interviews. It is of interest to note, however, that a significant fraction of the long-term cases, about 15 to 20 percent, obtain 95 or more interviews before closing.

## 2. Sources of Referral

In the earlier years of the agency's operation, social agencies were by far the most important single source of referral of clients, accounting for almost 40 percent of all referrals. They are still a major source and have diminished in relative importance only as reapplications became significant, rising from about 3 percent in 1958 to 15 to 20 percent within the last seven years, and as referrals by other ALCS clients rose from about 5 percent to 13 to 14 percent. In addition to social agencies, individual social workers and physicians and psychiatrists have been important referral sources, each accounting for about 12 to 15 percent of referrals. In the last full year of operation, these five sources—social agencies, social workers, physicians and psychiatrists, ALCS clients and reapplications—were the source of four-fifths of all referrals. The remainder, as in earlier years, came from lawyers, schools, religious organizations and clergy, and others. Referrals by ALCS clients and reapplications accounted for between one-fourth and one-third of all referrals during the last five years.

### 3. Previous Psychiatric or Social Agency Treatment

While social agencies have been a major source of referral of clients to ALCS, only a small percentage of ALCS clients had previously been treated by a social agency—never more than 17 to 18 percent in the earliest years, and more recently not more than around 10 percent. On the other hand, more than one-third of the clients have had previous psychiatric treatment, a proportion which has been fairly stable in the last ten years. Perhaps most interesting of all, however, is that in most years more than half the clients had had no previous experience with either social agency or psychiatric treatment or with any other nonmedical therapist.

### 4. Place of Clients' Residence

As would be expected, ALCS, located in Manhattan, draws most of its clientele from New York City. The proportion has ranged from 73 to 81 percent during the last ten years. Most of the rest came from nearby areas in New York State and New Jersey, but a few came from Connecticut and other states. While the proportion of clients who reside in the city varies to some extent from year to year, basically it is the residence of three-quarters of ALCS clients.

### 5. Marital Status

About three-quarters of ALCS clients are married. The remainder are divided more or less equally among single individuals and those who are divorced, widowed or separated. The variations in the relative size of each group among the total client caseload from year to year do not appear to be significant.

## 6.  Client Problems

The classification of problem area is broad and revealing only of the
very general nature of the problem, i.e., marital, pre-marital, parent-
child, etc. Reflecting the marital status of the bulk of the clients,
marital difficulties are the problem for 40 to 50 percent of the clients
and parent-child relationships for another 20 to 25 percent. Most of
the remainder, presumably among those who are single, divorced,
separated or widowed, are classified as emotional and personal.

## 7.  Education of Head of Client Household

ALCS clients are in general an educated group. With few exceptions,
all clients have at least graduated from high school and more than two-
fifths have graduated from college, including about one-fifth who have
done some graduate work. What is interesting and curious, however,
is that the proportion of college graduates among ALCS clients has
been *declining* over the years. It ranged between 68 and 80 percent in
1955-56 to 1957-58, dropped to around 60 percent for several years
in the early sixties, then went below 60 percent for a few years, and
in the last four years of operation, ranged from 42 to 47 percent. An
appropriate explanation does not come easily to mind, but it may reflect a change toward a more favorable attitude toward casework
counseling in the ALCS setting among the less well educated (that
is, the high school graduate) though well-to-do population in the city.

## 8.  Occupational Characteristics of Clients

Reflecting the generally high educational levels, ALCS clients are
heavily concentrated in professional, technical and similar occupations
(about 40 percent) and among managers, officials and proprietors
(35 to 40 percent). About 20 percent are sales or clerical workers or
are skilled or unskilled workers. The year-to-year changes do not show
any particular trends in the relative size of the various occupational
groupings among the agency's clients.

## 9.  Income Distribution of Clients

ALCS has been able to obtain from most of its clients information
on their annual incomes even though—or possibly because—there is no
relationship between the client's income and the fee he pays. A proportion, varying from less than 10 percent in some years to a bit
more than one-third in other years, have not wished to disclose their

income. Thus the data on income distribution must be viewed with some caution and little significance can be attached to year-to-year changes. Nevertheless, it can be stated with certainty that the agency's clientele is drawn, in the main, from the better off income groups. The median income of ALCS clients during the years 1966-67 to 1968-69 ranged between $17,000 and almost $20,000; the median income of white families in New York City in 1968 was $9,623. [5] In these same years, from one-half to two-thirds of ALCS clients had annual incomes between $15,000 and $35,000. On the other hand, the less affluent, those with incomes below $15,000, also had sub-stantial representation among the agency's clients, constituting, on average, about two-fifths of all clients.

Unpublished data made available by one of the major philan-thropic family service agencies in New York make it clear that ALCS clients are indeed drawn from a higher income and occupational group than is the clientele of the voluntary agencies. The median annual in-come in 1966-67 to 1968-69 of the voluntary agency clients was from $6,500 to $7,540 compared to the ALCS median of $17,000 to $20,000. Further, while from one-half to two-thirds of ALCS clients in recent years had annual incomes between $15,000 and $35,000, only about 4 to 8 percent of the voluntary agency clients had incomes of $15,000 or more and only a handful of these were above $20,000. A similar contrast can be noted with respect to occupational dis-tribution: 75 percent of ALCS clients came from the professional, technical group or from proprietors, managers and officials, com-pared to 27 percent of the voluntary agency clients. In sum, both ALCS and the philanthropically supported voluntary agency are ful-filling their function. ALCS is serving those who can afford to pay the cost of the service, the voluntary agency is serving, by and large, those who cannot afford to pay the full cost of counseling.

NOTES

1. The word *surplus* is used here and in several other places in this memorandum. It should be noted that the agency did not have a true surplus but rather an excess of income over expenditures which was placed in a contingency fund to provide for unexpected drains on income and expenses involved in the possible termination of the agency.

2. Beginning in 1961, the first year the agency moved from a

deficit to a surplus position and through 1963, the agency did not change the caseworker salary. Instead, it made an adjustment at the end of the year on the basis of the surplus which had accrued during the year. Subsequently this method was abandoned in favor of increments in salary.

3.   Blanche Bernstein, "Income Distribution in New York City," *The Public Interest* (July 1970).

4.   The fee for an individual interview was $17.50 from February 1, 1966 until March 1, 1969, when it was raised to $22.50.

5.   Blanche Bernstein, op. cit.


### TABLE I
### TOTAL NUMBER OF INTERVIEWS EACH YEAR
### 1954-55 through 1968-69

| | |
|---|---|
| 1954-55 | 1,472 |
| 1955-56 | 3,481 |
| 1956-57 | 4,195½ |
| 1957-58 | 5,808½ |
| 1958-59 | 7,383½ |
| 1959-60 | 8,893 |
| 1960-61 | 10,396¼ |
| 1961-62 | 11,679 |
| 1962-63 | 11,640⅓ |
| 1963-64 | 12,493 |
| 1964-65 | 11,851⅓ |
| 1965-66 | 11,352⅓ |
| 1966-67 | 11,514⅔ |
| 1967-68 | 11,260⅔ |
| 1968-69 | 10,470 |
| | |
| *All years* | 133,891 |

## TABLE II

### NUMBER AND PERCENT DISTRIBUTION OF CASES CLOSED, BY CATEGORIES, 1955–1969

| Year ending June 30 | Total closed | BSA (tel. only) | | BSB (1 interview) | | CSA (2-5 interviews) | | CSB (6 or more) | |
|---|---|---|---|---|---|---|---|---|---|
| | | Number | Percent | Number | Percent | Number | Percent | Number | Percent |
| 1955 | 264 | 118 | 45% | 72 | 27% | 54 | 20% | 20 | 8% |
| 1956 | 394 | 148 | 38 | 100 | 25 | 66 | 17 | 80 | 20 |
| 1957 | 373 | 210 | 56 | 61 | 16 | 49 | 13 | 53 | 14 |
| 1958 | 599 | 339 | 56 | 67 | 11 | 69 | 12 | 124 | 21 |
| 1959 | 583 | 313 | 54 | 97 | 16 | 69 | 12 | 104 | 18 |
| 1960 | 654 | 278 | 42 | 103 | 16 | 95 | 15 | 178 | 27 |
| 1961 | 554 | 293 | 53 | 73 | 13 | 61 | 11 | 127 | 23 |
| 1962 | 551 | 283 | 51 | 55 | 10 | 70 | 13 | 143 | 26 |
| 1963 | 548 | 223 | 41 | 74 | 13 | 75 | 14 | 176 | 32 |
| 1964 | 570 | 264 | 46 | 55 | 10 | 80 | 14 | 171 | 30 |
| 1965 | 512 | 208 | 41 | 70 | 14 | 77 | 15 | 157 | 30 |
| 1966 | 571 | 273 | 48 | 76 | 13 | 87 | 15 | 135 | 24 |
| 1967 | 453 | 198 | 44 | 77 | 17 | 63 | 14 | 115 | 25 |
| 1968 | 493 | 212 | 43 | 71 | 14 | 48 | 10 | 162 | 33 |
| 1969 | 459 | 211 | 46 | 39 | 8 | 76 | 17 | 133 | 29 |

## TABLE III

### NUMBER OF INTERVIEWS
### FOR CSA AND CSB CLOSINGS, 1957–69

|                         | *CSA closings*          |                                  | *CSB closings*          |                                  |
| ----------------------- | ----------------------- | -------------------------------- | ----------------------- | -------------------------------- |
| Year ending June 30     | Number of closings      | Median number of interviews      | Number of closings      | Median number of interviews      |
| 1957 | 49 | 4.0 | 53  | 17 |
| 1958 | 69 | 3.8 | 124 | 17 |
| 1959 | 69 | 2.6 | 104 | 22 |
| 1960 | 95 | 3.3 | 178 | 16 |
| 1961 | 61 | 2.7 | 127 | 18 |
| 1962 | 70 | 2.5 | 143 | 23 |
| 1963 | 75 | 2.4 | 176 | 23 |
| 1964 | 80 | 2.3 | 171 | 27 |
| 1965 | 77 | 2.4 | 157 | 29 |
| 1966 | 87 | 2.5 | 135 | 24 |
| 1967 | 63 | 2.1 | 115 | 19 |
| 1968 | 48 | 2.3 | 162 | 26 |
| 1969 | 76 | 2.3 | 133 | 28 |

TABLE IV

PERCENT DISTRIBUTION, BY REFERRAL SOURCE, OF BSB, CSA, AND CSB CLOSINGS, 1955–69

| Year ending June 30 | Total BSB, CSA, & CSB closings | Social agency | Social worker* | Physicians & psychiatrists | Lawyers | Schools | Religious organizations | ALCS clients | Reapplications | Psychologists** | Other*** |
|---|---|---|---|---|---|---|---|---|---|---|---|
| 1955 | 146 | 39 | (a) | (a) | (a) | 6 | (a) | (a) | (a) | (a) | (a) |
| 1956 | 246 | 37 | 10 | 11 | 4 | 6 | 2 | 5 | 3 | 8 | 14 |
| 1957 | 163 | 31 | 15 | 12 | 3 | 7 | 4 | 7 | 3 | 4 | 14 |
| 1958 | 260 | 35 | 15 | 15 | 2 | 3 | 5 | 4 | 3 | 3 | 15 |
| 1959 | 270 | 23.4 | 14.8 | 15.6 | 3.9 | 2.7 | 3.5 | 5.5 | 10.9 | 3.9 | 15.8 |
| 1960 | 376 | 34.5 | 16.7 | 14 | 3 | 3.6 | 2 | 8.4 | 12.2 | 1.1 | 8.3 |
| 1961 | 261 | 29 | 18 | 13.9 | 2 | 7 | 1.3 | 9.3 | 12 | 1.7 | 5.8 |
| 1962 | 268 | 28 | 15 | 13 | 6 | 4 | 3 | 9 | 13 | 2 | 7 |
| 1963 | 325 | 26 | 16.4 | 12.1 | 5.1 | 6 | 1.6 | 9 | 14.5 | 1.8 | 7.5 |
| 1964 | 306 | 22 | 20 | 12.6 | 4 | 3.4 | 2 | 9.5 | 20 | 1 | 5.5 |
| 1965 | 304 | 24 | 17 | 14 | 5 | 3 | 1 | 11 | 18 | 1 | 6 |
| 1966 | 298 | 24 | 17 | 14.5 | 7 | 4 | 1 | 10 | 16.7 | 3 | 2.8 |
| 1967 | 255 | 33 | 13 | 9.5 | 2.4 | 5.3 | 2.4 | 10.2 | 16 | 3.5 | 4.7 |
| 1968 | 281 | 30.4 | 13.5 | 13.4 | 3.4 | 2.6 | 1.5 | 14 | 15.4 | .6 | 5.2 |
| 1969 | 248 | 22 | 12.2 | 12.1 | 6.1 | 3.3 | 1.2 | 13 | 20 | 1 | 9.1 |

(a) A less detailed classification was used during the first year. It showed 26% referred by psychiatrists, physicians, social workers and lawyers; 15% by private individuals, former clients, and board members; and 14% came to ALCS in response to newspapers and brochure.

*"Social worker" referral here means personal (friend, family) rather than agency related. **Nonmedical therapists, including psychologists, AAMC. ***Includes private individuals, board members.

## TABLE V

### PERCENT DISTRIBUTION, CASES CLOSED, 1955–69
### PREVIOUS PSYCHIATRIC
### OR SOCIAL AGENCY TREATMENT

| Year ending June 30 | Psychiatric only | Social agency only | Both psych. & social agency | Non-medical therapist | Neither |
|---|---|---|---|---|---|
| 1955 | 26 | 11 | 6 | | 57 |
| 1956 | 27 | 11 | 5 | | 57 |
| 1957 | 26 | 4 | 5 | | 65 |
| 1958 | 35 | 11 | 7 | | 47 |
| 1959 | 35 | 8 | 6 | | 51 |
| 1960 | 32.3 | 9.3 | 7.5 | | 50.9 |
| 1961 | 35 | 10 | 3 | | 52 |
| 1962 | 34 | 9 | 3 | 4 | 50 |
| 1963 | 34.5 | 7.2 | 7.5 | 2.5 | 48.3 |
| 1964 | 36 | 7.8 | 6.2 | 3 | 47 |
| 1965 | 33.8 | 8.5 | 3.9 | 4.2 | 49.6 |
| 1966 | 32 | 5.6 | 3.9 | 4.5 | 54 |
| 1967 | 31 | 4.3 | 4 | 2.7 | 58 |
| 1968 | 34.1 | 5.3 | 5.6 | 2.3 | 52.7 |
| 1969 | 36.2 | 4.4 | 3.4 | 4.4 | 51.6 |

## TABLE VI

### PERCENT DISTRIBUTION, BY PLACE OF RESIDENCE, OF BSB, CSA AND CSB CLOSINGS, 1955–69

| Year ending June 30 | Total BSB, CSA & CSB closings | Residence | | | | |
|---|---|---|---|---|---|---|
| | | N.Y. City | N.Y. State | N.J. | Conn. | Other |
| 1955 | 146 | 71 | 22 | 5 | 2 | |
| 1956 | 246 | 67 | 23 | 8 | 2 | |
| 1957 | 163 | 70 | 16 | 8 | 6 | |
| 1958 | 260 | 71 | 18 | 9 | 2 | |
| 1959 | 270 | 68 | 12 | 11 | 9 | |
| 1960 | 376 | 75.7 | 14.9 | 6 | 1.8 | 1.6 |
| 1961 | 261 | 80.4 | 8 | 9 | 2.3 | .3 |
| 1962 | 268 | 74.6 | 15.6 | 9.3 | .5 | |
| 1963 | 325 | 77 | 11.7 | 9.2 | 2.1 | |
| 1964 | 306 | 77.4 | 12.7 | 6.5 | 2.4 | 1 |
| 1965 | 304 | 78 | 12 | 6 | 2 | 2 |
| 1966 | 298 | 79.5 | 12.5 | 6 | 1.4 | .6 |
| 1967 | 255 | 72.5 | 13.7 | 11.8 | .8 | 1.2 |
| 1968 | 281 | 80.8 | 10.7 | 6.8 | .7 | 1 |
| 1969 | 248 | 76.6 | 10 | 11 | .8 | 1.6 |

## TABLE VII

### PERCENT DISTRIBUTION, BY MARITAL STATUS, OF BSB, CSA, AND CSB CLOSINGS, 1955–69

| Year ending June 30 | Total BSB, CSA & CSB closings | Married couple | Single | Divorced widowed or separated | Other |
|---|---|---|---|---|---|
| 1955 | 146 | 74 | 15 | 11 | |
| 1956 | 246 | 78 | 10 | 12 | |
| 1957 | 163 | 68 | 15 | 17 | |
| 1958 | 260 | 74 | 16 | 10 | |
| 1959 | 270 | 73 | 12 | 15 | |
| 1960 | 376 | 77.9 | 10.1 | 12 | |
| 1961 | 261 | 77 | 12 | 11 | |
| 1962 | 268 | 72 | 15 | 13 | |
| 1963 | 325 | 75.1 | 10.5 | 14.4 | |
| 1964 | 306 | 76.4 | 13.4 | 10.2 | |
| 1965 | 304 | 73 | 10 | 17 | |
| 1966 | 298 | 79.5 | 6.5 | 14 | |
| 1967 | 255 | 76.8 | 10.2 | 12.5 | .5 * |
| 1968 | 281 | 73.6 | 14 | 12 | .4 * |
| 1969 | 248 | 71.8 | 14.1 | 14.1 | |

* Unmarried couple

TABLE VIII

PERCENT DISTRIBUTION, BY PROBLEM AREA,
OF BSB, CSA, AND CSB CLOSINGS, 1955–69

| Year ending June 30 | Marital | Pre-marital | Parent-child | Emotional & personal | Other |
|---|---|---|---|---|---|
| 1955 | 41 | 5 | 25 | 9 | 20 |
| 1956 | 54 | 6 | 21 | 6 | 13 |
| 1957 | 47 | 9 | 28 | 4 | 12 |
| 1958 | 49 | 4 | 22 | 11 | 14 |
| 1959 | 50 | 4 | 24 | 14 | 8 |
| 1960 | 49 | 3 | 29 | 15 | 4 |
| 1961 | 48 | 5 | 29 | 14 | 4 |
| 1962 | 49 | 6 | 22 | 15 | 8 |
| 1963 | 50 | 4 | 23 | 15 | 8 |
| 1964 | 44.4 | 3 | 26 | 21.4 | 5.2 |
| 1965 | 51.3 | 3.2 | 20 | 21 | 4.5 |
| 1966 | 48.7 | 3 | 23.4 | 23 | 1.9 |
| 1967 | 51 | 4.3 | 26.2 | 16.5 | 2 |
| 1968 | 50 | 3.2 | 20 | 23.1 | 3.7 |
| 1969 | 41.1 | 3.2 | 23.8 | 27.5 | 4.4 |

## TABLE IX

### PERCENT DISTRIBUTION, BY EDUCATION OF HEAD OF HOUSEHOLD, OF BSB, CSA, AND CSB CLOSINGS, 1956–69

| Year ending June 30 | Post-graduate work | College | High school |
|---|---|---|---|
| 1956 | (na) | 80 | 97 |
| 1957 | (na) | 73 | 100 |
| 1958 | (na) | 68 | 98.5 |
| 1959 | 9.4 | 60.7 | 98.1 |
| 1960 | 12.7 | 61.1 | 95.9 |
| 1961 | 15 | 60 | 96 |
| 1962 | 26 | 65.5 | 96.5 |
| 1963 | 16.4 | 58.4 | 94.4 |
| 1964 | 23.5 | 58.8 | 94.3 |
| 1965 | 24 | 57 | 95 |
| 1966 | 17.4 | 41.8 | 95.2 |
| 1967 | 26.6 | 45 | 97 |
| 1968 | 18 | 47.1 | 96.6 |
| 1969 | 24 | 41.6 | 98.5 |

(na) not available

## TABLE X

### PERCENT DISTRIBUTION, BY OCCUPATION, OF BSB, CSA, AND CSB CLOSINGS, SELECTED YEARS, 1955–69

| Year ending June 30 | Professional, technical or kindred workers | Managers, officials, proprietors | Sales workers | Clerical workers | Skilled workers | Unskilled workers | Other |
|---|---|---|---|---|---|---|---|
| 1955 | 47 | 17 | 12 | 12 | (na) | (na) | (na) |
| 1956 | 34 | 28 | 11 | 18 | 6 | 1.4 | 3 |
| 1960 | 37.7 | 32.3 | 9.1 | 10.2 | 4.4 | 2 | 5 |
| 1961 | 38.7 | 35.8 | 7.7 | 7.3 | 5.3 | 1 | 3.2 |
| 1962 | 44 | 30 | 12 | 7 | 3 | .9 | 3 |
| 1963 | 38.5 | 33.3 | 9.7 | 7.4 | 4.2 | .6 | 6 |
| 1964 | 35 | 39.1 | 8.4 | 6 | .3 | * | 7.9 |
| 1965 | 40 | 30 | 11 | 6 | 7 | 3 | 6 |
| 1966 | 36 | 34.5 | 9 | 7.5 | 4 | 1.8 | 6 |
| 1967 | 42.4 | 35.1 | 2.2 | 7.2 | 6.3 |  | 5 |
| 1968 | 36.4 | 35.4 | 7.3 | 7.3 | 4.6 | 1.8 | 9 |
| 1969 | 40 | 37.8 | 6 | 5.4 | 3.6 | 1.8 | 5.4 |

(na) not available     *less than .5%

## TABLE XI
### PERCENTAGE INCOME DISTRIBUTION OF BSB, CSA, AND CSB CLOSINGS, 1962–69

| Fiscal Years | 1962 | 1963 | 1964 | 1965 | 1966 | 1967 | 1968 | 1969 |
|---|---|---|---|---|---|---|---|---|
| Total Cases | 268 | 325 | 306 | 304 | 298 | 255 | 281 | 248 |
| Income Unknown | 21 | 35 | 35 | 89 | 94 | 94 | 25 | 94 |
| Income Known | 247 | 290 | 271 | 215 | 204 | 161 | 256 | 154 |
| Income Known (%) | 100.0 | 100.0 | 100.0 | 100.0 | 100.0 | 100.0 | 100.0 | 100.0 |
| Under $3,000 | .9 | .6 | .3 | 1.9 | – | – | 2.0 | – |
| $3,000–5,999 | 8.5 | 7.6 | 9.6 | 9.3 | 6.4 | 6.2 | 5.5 | 3.9 |
| $6,000–8,999 | 18.2 | 12.8 | 10.3 | 14.8 | 15.2 | 13.7 | 9.8 | 5.8 |
| $9,000–11,999 | 21.9 | 17.9 | 18.5 | 14.8 | 16.2 | 11.8 | 13.6 | 11.6 |
| $12,000–14,999 | 11.7 | 13.4 | 12.2 | 15.8 | 13.1 | 10.6 | 11.7 | 8.5 |
| $15,000–19,999 | 17.0 | 19.7 | 21.8 | 14.9 | 15.7 | 17.4 | 21.9 | 21.5 |
| $20,000–24,999 | 21.8 | 10.7 | 9.2 | 11.3 | 11.8 | 16.8 | 13.7 | 17.6 |
| $25,000–29,999 | – | 15.9 | 5.9 | 6.0 | 7.4 | 8.6 | 10.5 | 9.1 |
| $30,000–34,999 | – | – | 4.1 | 7.4 | 8.3 | 8.1 | 9.8 | 14.3 |
| Over $35,000 | – | 1.4 | 8.1 | 3.8 | 5.9 | 6.8 | 1.5 | 7.7 |
| Median Income (Current Dollars) | $12,129 | $14,484 | $14,778 | $13,746 | $14,793 | $18,630 | $16,690 | $19,695 |
| Median Income (Constant 1968–1969 Dollars) | $14,701 | $17,242 | $17,264 | $16,002 | $16,602 | $20,316 | $17,568 | $19,695 |

# Appendix IV

*Report of the*
*Ad Hoc Committee on Private Practice*
November 30, 1966

The Committee on Private Practice recommends for Board action the following policy regarding ALCS staff engaging in private practice:

> The determination to carry private practice shall be a personal and individual one. It is assumed that the mature professional person makes such determination within the context of fulfilling basic responsibilities to the ALCS. This applies to all forms of private practice, whether it be in casework counseling, teaching, consultation, or other professional activity.

The Committee's recommendation is based upon the following premises:

> (1) The ALCS staff were selected and expected to function as mature professional persons. (One of the concepts upon which ALCS is based is that full professional maturity occurs where the opportunity for such responsibility exists.) The ALCS concept of full professional maturity involves not only responsibility for service to clients but also responsibility for the financing of the agency.

> (2) The management of private practice in casework counseling has added value for the development of pro-

fessional competence and maturity. The ALCS encourages each staff member to assume full responsibility for the service he gives to ALCS clients. We have experienced at ALCS that such responsibility does create added incentive for continuing professional development. However, this practice is carried on within an organizational setup. Private practice places the caseworker in a situation where he is judged solely on his own merits. Therefore, there is reason to believe that this may create even further incentive for professional development.

(3) One of the hallmarks of professional maturity is the caseworker's ability to evaluate his practice and to determine the areas in which he requires some additional knowledge or experience. To achieve this, he may decide to undertake a new form of professional practice (teaching, group therapy, or offering consultation to agencies). Others may decide to take additional training in advanced professional seminars or in some related field. Others may decide to engage in the private practice of casework. As the individual benefits from his experience, so does the agency totally.

(4) The agency experience with those who are on the regular staff and who have had private practice in counseling indicates that they conduct their private practice within the context of fulfilling ALCS responsibilities, since they are committed to the agency and its goals.

The Committee recommends that the staff consider the basic ALCS responsibilities and determine where additional clarification or interpretation is needed in view of the possible adoption of the policy by the Board.

Mrs. Benjamin J. Buttenwieser
Msgr. Francis J. Mugavero
Miss Alice Fine
Mr. Rubin Blanck

Guest Participants: Mr. Joseph P. Anderson
Miss Rena Schulman

*Staff Recommendations to Accompany the*
*Recommendations of the Committee*
*on Private Practice*
November 30, 1966

In response to the recommendation of the Committee on Private Practice and in the knowledge that staff shares with Board responsibility for the financial stability of the agency, the staff reviewed basic ALCS responsibilities in order to determine what safeguards would be needed if the Committee's recommendation on private practice is adopted by the Board. The staff agreed that:

> (1) The minimum interviews required for each staff member be defined on the basis of the number required to meet the financial needs of the agency, rather than, as at present, on the number required to earn base salary.

> (2) At any point that a staff member decides that he will build his private practice toward the goal of ending his connection at ALCS, he will inform the group of his intention. This will allow for responsible advance planning for his replacement and withdrawal, thus assuring the preservation of the financial structure of the agency.

Since staff members engaging in private practice desire the experience of more total reliance on themselves and their competence, it is assumed that they will develop their own sources of referral, will not exploit their connection with ALCS in any announcement of their availability for referrals or in any self-promotion, and will determine their own fees.

The ALCS will not normally refer clients to the private practice of individual staff members. Where exceptions to this policy seem indicated (such as if a member of the immediate family of a staff person or Board member requires help), referrals will be made through the Executive Director. The fee in such instances will not be less than the ALCS fee (currently $25.00 an hour)*. The same fee will be the minimum where a staff member is recommended to take on a teaching or consultation request made of the agency.

Persons who join ALCS staff and are already in private practice

---

* [The $17.50 fee was for a 45-minute interview. — R.F.]

or desire to enter into it will be informed *during the hiring process* of the basic responsibilities involved in becoming a member of ALCS and how these affect his private practice. It has been the group's experience that new staff members require a period of time, however, to understand fully the relationship of staff to total agency operation. This process seems to take about a year. Therefore, the staff recommends that even the exceptional referral will not be made to new staff members during this period.

It is assumed that evening staff (that is, those members of staff who do not carry responsibility for the administration and financial soundness of ALCS) will not be interested in private practice. The ALCS serves as the source of additional professional activity for this group. However, should this assumption be incorrect, the ALCS would not refer to them under any circumstances.

These recommendations and the overall policy, if adopted, will be reviewed after a year's experience to see whether any changes or new recommendations need to be made. A report of the follow-up will be presented to the Board.

# Appendix V

*Report of Technical Advisory Committee
to Board of Directors*
October 30, 1963

The Technical Advisory Committee has maintained close identity with the ALCS since its inception nine years ago. During the past year we have devoted our attention to assessing the program in relation to its purpose and goals, and to filtering from the experience implications for other social agencies and for the field of social work.

We believe the ALCS has clearly demonstrated that casework services can be successfully offered to people unaccustomed to using social agencies, and that such services can become self-supporting. We wish, at the outset of this report, to congratulate the Board on its vision and courage in undertaking and developing this pilot demonstration which has served already, in our opinion, to strengthen the status of social casework. We are appreciative of the creativity and innovation that have distinquished the program, whose findings have been followed closely by a significant segment of the leadership in our field. We wish to lend our full support to the preparation and distribution of an account of the ALCS experience to the field of social work, and to assist the Board in developing a new program for further experimentation in this same area.

## I. Report to the Field of Social Work

Provision of professional services developed in and offered through social agencies has been extended to a widening segment of the population. The earlier exclusive identification of social work with the

223

needs of economically deprived groups has given way to professional acceptance of the fact that all people in all walks of life may and often do face both economic need and problems in human relations which call for professional social work help.

That we have as a nation developed so much more rapidly our provision for extending basic economic security for all than we have in extending professional counseling and other casework services designed to preserve and strengthen family life, stems from a variety of social, economic and political factors, and is related to developments within the social work profession itself. The present direction of national policy toward extending and improving professional counseling and other social services under governmental auspices or subsidy is encouraging. With the further development of professionally staffed public services, the voluntary agencies may have the opportunity of reshaping some of their programs and services. Some may wish to consider ways and means of extending professional help through new structures and promoting a variety of preventive services. There is general acknowledgment of the need to extend the quantity of casework service in the interest of community health.

Social work's traditional and present commitment is to helping the poor—the disadvantaged; but no profession can ethically withhold its services from a particular segment of the population. Those of us who serve on the Technical Advisory Committee are committed to the proposition that casework services should be available to the *entire* community, and believe that the field will welcome ideas and methods designed to accomplish this without either adding to the quest for voluntary funds or curtailing subsidized services for the needy.

We believe the experience of the ALCS over the past nine years to be an important extension of experience accruing in other social agencies, and that it offers to the field of social work a valuable frame of reference in this regard.

The ALCS has been self-supporting on the basis of fees for the past two years. It has been able to set aside a sum of money each year to develop a contingency fund as a guarantee of safeguarding services to clients through possible periods of unexpected emergencies. Such safeguards are seen as an essential part of treatment responsibilities to clients.

At the same time, the ALCS has been able to offer casework services to clients at a reasonable fee, maintain sound professional standards, guarantee good personnel practices to its staff, and has given them adequate compensation.

We believe that the ALCS experience has applicability to a portion of the clients served by casework agencies and to a portion of the functions carried by such agencies. We would like to make the following observations:

A. A fixed fee, covering the full cost of service, is a departure from traditional agency practice. Some agencies utilize a sliding scale for fees, which ranges from a free service to a fee exceeding cost. We believe the time has come to examine our practice in this area and we propose the following hypothesis:

*A fixed fee, reflecting full cost of casework service and charged to persons able to meet it is one way of assuring that extension of such services to the middle- and upper-income group does not detract from the volume or quality of such services for people who cannot afford such payment.*

We believe that utilizing, interpreting and publicizing a new fee structure would serve to:

1) Enable social agencies to employ fully philanthropic funds for services required by those who cannot pay for their full cost.

2) Clarify for the contributing community the programs which gifts support or subsidize.

3) Clarify for clients and potential clients their status as paying or subsidized consumers.

B. One of the premises upon which the ALCS was built was that there existed a segment of the middle- and upper-income group who would use the services now offered by casework agencies if these could be obtained upon the same basis as other professional services. The basis was defined as meaning the fixed fee related to full cost of service, and an experienced staff as well as congenial physical surroundings.

*We believe that these distinctive features of the ALCS have facilitated the use of social service offered at the ALCS for a new group of clients. We believe that it is possible, therefore, that if these same distinctive features could be introduced into the structure of existing casework agencies, they, too, would attract a wider upper- and middle-income clientele than they have to date.*

In examining the effect of these distinctive features upon the success of the ALCS which have applicability for agencies wishing to attract the same clientele, we have identified the following areas of agreement:

1) The fixed fee covering the cost of service affords the opportunity for placing emphasis upon the professional aspect of the service rather than upon its philanthropic basis, and hence stimulates its use by the middle- and upper-income group.

2) Persons in this group are apt to be *initially attracted* as clients of casework agencies when given assurance that they will be served by qualified and competent staff. Such staff is best able to project the degree of professional competence required to attract and later hold this particular clientele.

3) A separate facility, located in an area of the community comparable to the natural environs of the clientele, will encourage applications from this new client group.

4) A public interpretation program is necessary to project the service as one for the use of middle- and upper-income groups rather than as one deserving their financial support.

C. In addition to the above observations, which might have implications for existing agencies, we believe a report of the ALCS experience would have meaning to communities wishing to establish a *new agency* to serve this clientele. Whether such a program as that developed by ALCS should be offered within an existing casework agency or in a new and separate structure will depend upon a variety of individual community circumstances. We have identified the following:

1) *The availability of the range of services traditionally offered by casework agencies.*

The limited function of ALCS (both as regards clients served and services offered) is made possible by the availability of such community programs as subsidized casework, homemaker placement, and day care services, social affairs activity, etc.

2) *The availability of specialists such as home econo-mists, psychiatrists, and psychologists for consultations.*

3) The size of the middle- and upper-income group and its degree of sophistication with regard to the values of utilizing professional help with personal and family problems.

**D.** These are our observations and the areas of general applicability which we have been able to identify. In order for readers to accept, debate, or extend them, it will be necessary for the report to contain a full description of the agency and a factual account of the experience to date.

We propose that the report include the following:

1) A statement of the purpose and goals of the program.

2) The structure of the agency.

3) A description of the physical plant.

4) A delineation of the policies and procedures inaug-urated to attract the particular clientele. These would include: fixed fee, staff qualifications, consultative ser-vices, expansion of program as needed to meet requests for service, etc., and the program of public interpreta-tion.

5) Demographic material which describes the clientele—its characteristics, rate of application and sources of referral, and presenting problems. In addition, we be-lieve that the field would be interested in knowing the ALCS experience with waiting lists.

6) The policies and professional activities developed to foster and safeguard sound professional practice. These should include full information about personnel policies, employment practices, opportunities for professional development, peer consultation, and evaluatory pro-cesses, including recording.

7) An account of the policies and procedures which have led to agency self-support. These would include the following: financial structure, production expecta-tions of staff, and method of implementation, fee setting and collecting, financial compensation of staff, includ-ing salaries, bonus and the opportunity to earn extra

payment for interviews carried in excess of the basic requirement.

*We believe that the ALCS experience points up the importance of having staff know the financial structure of the agency, and understand the relationship between unit service costs and production requirements for self-support.* The Technical Advisory Committee believes that the ALCS policies which state basic production expectations and provide an incentive of money payment for higher production have been central to agency self-support and have doubtless influenced staff stability. It would, we believe, be interesting to the field to know that only five staff members have resigned in the nine years of operation, and that of this number, three left to work in other social agencies, one to be married, and one to enter private practice.

We consider the achievement of staff partnership as essential to agency self-support but would like to observe other experiments in order to clarify whether or not the necessity of agency self-support is an essential ingredient to achieving such partnership and staff maturity.

8) We would hope that the report could include some assessment by the Board as to the differences or similarities of their expectations, contributions, and investment in serving to launch and maintain a self-supporting rather than a philanthropic service. Their identification of differences, of problems, or of rewards, would have value to other agencies and communities as they seek to develop citizen support for such programs.

## II.  *Future Program*

The ALCS program is assuredly successful. We cannot, however, state definitively the specific constellation of ingredients which have been essential to this success, nor can we be sure that the same formula would produce equally good results in other communities or under different conditions. For example, it may not be possible in some communities to employ staff as highly experienced as that available to ALCS. Could the required supervision costs in such an instance be offset by a salary differential? Is the comparable level of practice required for peer consultation a necessary basis for the quality of staff partnership required for agency self-support? What social services, in addition to casework, might be required of such an agency located in a community having limited social services? For example, if a community has no resources available for the placement of an aged family member or for providing a homemaker when a parent must leave the home temporarily—how might these necessary services be incorporated into such a structure?

We support the Board's plan to stimulate and foster the development of casework services to persons in the middle- and upper-income groups and to experiment in a variety of structures and in different localities.

We suggest the following principles for incorporation into the planning of the future programs:

> **A.** *Financing. The ALCS Board might be prepared to provide initial financing ("seed money") to enable the service to be established* and secure its movement toward self-support.
>
> While some communities may have financial resources available for establishing such a program, many will not. The funds might be available on a free or loan basis—and a time limit should be established for their availability.
>
> **B.** *Types of Experimentation. The design of the project should be broad enough to encourage experimentation through a variety of structure and in a variety of localities.* Three possibilities are suggested:
>
>> 1) To help existing casework agencies develop or extend services to clients in the middle- and upper-income levels through a distinct unit or program within the agency.
>>
>> 2) To help existing casework agencies develop or extend such services by establishing a separate structure (this might be affiliated with one or more agencies, or might be independent).
>>
>> 3) To help communities having a substantial segment of citizens in the middle- and upper-income groups and no traditional family service agencies to establish a program like ALCS.
>>
>>> The latter possibility offers the opportunity to make the initial interpretation of social work to the

economically advantaged in the community as a service they will pay for and use, and it offers the hope that, after experiencing its benefits, they might wish to extend these to persons unable to pay full cost. Such a development might result in a more broadly based and financed social agency structure.

C. *Board Participation. Lay leadership is seen as essential to the development and interpretation of such a program in any community.* Traditional methods of selection and determination of role and responsibility will need examination in light of ALCS experience.

D. *Professional Advisory Committee. Professional leadership should be utilized,* either through board or committee membership.

E. *Professional Staff. Qualified staff is essential for the success of such projects.*
Problems are anticipated in locations outside metropolitan areas. Communities interested in developing such projects will need to understand and accept the personnel policies basic to attracting and holding qualified staff.

F. *Selecting Communities for Experimentation.* Examination of the Family Service Association of America standards governing membership might suggest components for measuring a community's readiness to engage in such a project.

In addition to the program above, the Technical Advisory Committee hopes that the Board will explore the possibility of developing a professional educational experiment with a school of social work. We believe it incumbent upon social agencies to support and participate in the educational process and believe the ALCS may have an important contribution to make at the doctorate level.

We look forward to the next phase of agency experimentation and pledge our interest and support. We believe the field of social work should be informed about plans for the future program and recommend that the report to the field contain a section setting forth its purpose.

| | |
|---|---|
| Herbert H. Aptekar | George Hallwachs |
| Frances L. Beatman | Frank J. Hertel |
| Clark W. Blackburn | Margaret Kaufman |
| Frederick I. Daniels | Rosemary Sheridan |
| Stanley P. Davies | Sanford N. Sherman |

THE TEXT for this book was composed by ESP, Inc., Nyack, New York 10960, using IBM Selectric Composer *Aldine Roman* type for the text proper and Univers for running heads, folios, and Index.

THE LAKESIDE PRESS of the R.R. Donnelley & Sons Company printed this book on its Cameron Belt Press, provided the patent ("perfect") binding, and produced the jacket at its Crawfordsville, Indiana plant.